HOW TO PASS

HIGHER

FRENCH

Douglas Angus

HODDER
GIBSON
AN HACHETTE UK COMPANY

Acknowledgements

The Publishers would like to thank the following for permission to reproduce copyright material:

Acknowledgements
Specimen Papers, Marking Instructions and extracts from the Arrangement Documents are reproduced by permission of the Scottish Qualifications Authority.

CD Acknowledgements
Voices: Fanny Chouc, Camille Jeanjot, Arnaud Richard and Julien Touzan.
Audio Engineering: Phil Booth, Heriot-Watt University.

Every effort has been made to trace all copyright holders, but if any have been inadvertently overlooked the Publishers will be pleased to make the necessary arrangements at the first opportunity.

Although every effort has been made to ensure that website addresses are correct at time of going to press, Hodder Gibson cannot be held responsible for the content of any website mentioned in this book. It is sometimes possible to find a relocated web page by typing in the address of the home page for a website in the URL window of your browser.

Hachette's policy is to use papers that are natural, renewable and recyclable products and made from wood grown in sustainable forests. The logging and manufacturing processes are expected to conform to the environmental regulations of the country of origin.

If the CD is missing from this package, please contact us on 0141 848 1609 or at hoddergibson@hodder.co.uk, advising where and when you purchased the book.

Orders: please contact Bookpoint Ltd, 130 Milton Park, Abingdon, Oxon OX14 4SB. Telephone: (44) 01235 827720. Fax: (44) 01235 400454. Lines are open 9.00–5.00, Monday to Saturday, with a 24-hour message answering service. Visit our website at www.hoddereducation.co.uk. Hodder Gibson can be contacted direct on: Tel: 0141 848 1609; Fax: 0141 889 6315; email: hoddergibson@hodder.co.uk

© Douglas Angus 2007
First published in 2007 by
Hodder Gibson, an imprint of Hodder Education,
an Hachette UK Company
2a Christie Street
Paisley PA1 1NB

Impression number   5 4 3

Year   2010

Cover photo SETE – illuminations Pierre Bideau
Illustrations by Richard Duszczak, Cartoon Studio
Typeset in 9.5 on 12.5pt Frutiger Light by Phoenix Photosetting, Chatham, Kent
Printed and bound in Great Britain by Martins The Printers, Berwick-upon-Tweed

A catalogue record for this title is available from the British Library

ISBN 978-0-340-92812-7

CONTENTS

Chapter 1

INTRODUCTION TO HIGHER FRENCH

Introduction to this book

This book is a guide to all the skill areas of Higher French, and to how to get the best possible mark in each area. There are separate sections giving advice on reading and translation, listening, speaking and writing. For reading and listening, there are also practice questions, with answers so that you can check your work. For speaking and writing, we work through some sample questions, looking at how to improve your performance in assessments. Accompanying this book is a CD of listening material, and in the book there are questions and transcripts to go with this CD, which are indicated in the book by the 💿 symbol.

What is involved in Higher French?

Higher French, like all your other Highers, is a course which is tested by a mixture of internal (Unit) and external (Course) assessment. Both of these assess the four skills of reading, listening, speaking and writing. There are two Units which make up your Higher, the Language Unit and the Optional Unit. The Language Unit is assessed by three NAB (National Assessment Bank) assessments, one in each of reading, speaking and listening. The Optional Unit (Reading and Viewing, or Language in Work) is assessed through your writing.

The Course is assessed in two ways. Three of the skills, reading, writing and listening, will be assessed at the end of the course in an external exam set and marked by the Scottish Qualifications Authority (SQA). What is new in Higher, as opposed to Intermediate or Standard Grade, is translation: you will be asked to translate a short extract of the reading passage from French into English.

The assessment of speaking is different from the other areas: it will be assessed by a presentation and conversation with your teacher, which will be recorded. Your teacher will give you a grade for this, and this will be your final grade, subject to moderation by SQA. That means your teacher may be asked to send the recording off to SQA to be moderated (checked), but in nearly all cases your teacher's mark will be your Higher mark. This speaking assessment will also double as your Unit assessment.

How is my final mark made up?

This is very straightforward. Your marks will also be your percentages. Your speaking is marked out of 25, so that is 25 per cent of your mark, and so on. This means:

◆ **Reading and translation:** this makes up 30 per cent of your mark; 20 marks are for the answers to the questions on the passage, 10 for the translation.

◆ **Writing:** you will be asked to write an account, in French, of a visit you have made to a French-speaking country. You will be asked to mention several specific details. This will be worth 15 marks.

◆ **Listening:** this is worth 20 marks. You will also have to write your own opinions on the topic of the Listening assessment in French. This writing will be worth 10 marks.

◆ **Speaking:** the marks you get for your presentation (up to 10 marks) and your conversation (up to 15 marks) are the final part of your total.

What do I have to know?

You will be expected to know all the basic vocabulary of Standard Grade, but also vocabulary related to each of the themes and topic areas of Higher, which are provided in a table in Appendix One. This will make listening and reading in French easier for you. In Chapter 14, we have reprinted the basic Standard Grade vocabulary to help you to revise, and have added useful vocabulary for Higher to this.

You will also need to know more about grammar than you did at Intermediate or Standard Grade, so that you can write and speak French at the appropriate level for Higher. The grammar grid in Appendix Two should give you an idea of what you are expected to know. Your writing should show you have some knowledge of grammar, and you must work at getting your structures and endings right. For speaking, also, your teacher and examiner will be looking for you to demonstrate a knowledge of structure, verbs and the other aspects of language set out in the grammar grid.

You must also be able to use a good dictionary, to help you to understand French in the reading and listening papers, and to let you find words you need for your speaking and writing. This means you need to know properly how your dictionary works, how to look up things quickly and how to interpret what you find when you have looked something up. You will find some advice on this in the reading section of this book.

What exactly is involved in the exam?

There are three parts to the exam: the first part will normally take place in February or March, and will be your Speaking assessment. The second and third parts are Paper 1 and Paper 2, which you will sit in May. Paper 1 lasts one hour and forty minutes, and is made up of Reading, Translation and Directed Writing. You will have to manage your time for this yourself. Paper 2 is Listening and Personal Response (opinion) Writing, and will last for one hour.

Speaking

Speaking will be assessed by your teacher and externally moderated by SQA, as explained on p. 1. What you talk about should be organised between you and your teacher.

You will have to carry out two tasks:

◆ A presentation to your teacher on a topic you choose (using notes of no more than 5 headings of up to 8 words each in English, or in French to support you). This should last about two minutes.

◆ A conversation with your teacher, starting on the same topic, which will then move on to other topic areas you have studied during your Higher course. This should last about five minutes.

While the presentation is something you have control of, you must be ready to carry on the conversation into other areas which will develop from the initial part of the conversation. However, remember it is a conversation, and you also can lead it where you want it to go. We will give you some advice on this in Chapter 10 (Speaking). This assessment will also double as your Unit assessment.

Listening

For the Course, listening will be assessed in Paper 2 of the external Higher examination. This will use a recording of a dialogue between two French speakers, and you will be asked to give answers based upon what you hear. This dialogue will last about two minutes, and you will hear it twice.

The questions will be set and answered in English, and will follow the order of the dialogue. You will be allowed to use a French dictionary, and we will give you advice on this in Chapter 6 (Listening).

The Unit Listening assessment is similar, but you will be able to hear the text three times rather than twice. For this assessment you will **not** be allowed to use a dictionary.

Reading and translation

The Course Reading paper is one longish text, of about 600 words, with questions which will be set and answered in English. You may well find unusual words translated for you in a glossary. You will be allowed to use a French dictionary, and will have to be good at using this, as otherwise you will spend so much time looking up words that you will never finish answering the questions!

One part of the reading text will be underlined (usually a short paragraph, or three to four sentences) and you will be asked to translate this into English.

For the Unit Reading assessment, there is no translation, and the text is shorter, of 400 to 450 words.

Writing

Writing will be assessed in three ways. First, you will have to carry out a Unit assessment based on your Optional Unit. This will be marked by your teacher. You will find more information on this in Chapter 13. You will also have to produce two pieces of writing in your external Higher exam:

◆ Directed Writing, of 150–180 words, which will be an account of a journey you have made;
◆ Personal Response Writing, of 120–150 words, which will be linked to the topic discussed in the Listening assessment.

For both of these pieces of writing you will be allowed a dictionary.

What grammar do I need to know?

When marking your work, teachers will be looking for a variety of different structures, a good level of accuracy in basic structures, and some control of more complex language. You will be allowed to make some errors, but this will affect the grade you are awarded.

HOW TO PASS HIGHER FRENCH

Verbs

You should

◆ use the correct form of the present, imperfect, perfect, future and conditional tenses, and use modal verbs correctly;

◆ use *ne . . . pas*, *ne . . . jamais*, etc.;

◆ use relative pronouns and conjunctions;

◆ know the irregular verbs.

Nouns and pronouns

You should

◆ use the correct type of article/determiner (a, the, this) and the correct form (e.g. correct gender or number);

◆ use the correct pronouns, and put them in the right place;

◆ use the correct plural forms.

For better grades, you will have to do more than this: the grammar grid in Appendix Two shows what markers are going to be looking for. When you are working towards Higher, you are expected to know everything covered at Intermediate level as well as the things which are marked for Higher level.

How do I go about learning vocabulary?

The best way to revise is to practise, although different people have different ways of learning vocabulary; the following ways might be useful to you.

1. Try writing out a list of words, then reading them out: cover up the French and see if you can remember it from the English, and of course the other way round.

2. Read things over several times, on different occasions.

3. Check your memorising, either by covering one part and remembering the other, or by getting someone to do it with you (a friend, or a parent). If you have someone who will help you, get him/her to say a word in English, which you have to put into French.

4. Try to get your words organised into areas, so they all hang together and make sense to you.

5. Use spidergrams of related words.

Chapter 14 lists the structures and vocabulary you can be expected to know under each topic, and Appendix One will give you an overview of the themes and topics of Higher French.

READING AND TRANSLATION

Introduction

Answering the questions in your Reading paper is worth **20 per cent** of your final mark in Higher French; you will also have to translate a short passage from the text you read into English, for a further **10 per cent**. You should allow about one hour to read the text, answer the questions and do the translation. The text will be about 600 words long. You will be able to use a dictionary for this exam, and so you need to be very confident about your dictionary use. As a Unit assessment, before you sit the final exam, you will also have to do a Reading NAB: this text will be at the same level of difficulty as the final exam, but the passage will be shorter – about 400 words long. You will not have to translate as part of the NAB assessment.

When you sit the exam, you will have one hour and forty minutes for the paper which includes Reading, Translation and the Directed Writing. It is up to you how to divide the time, and what order to do the paper in, but as a rough guideline you should spend no more than sixty minutes on the Reading and Translation, and no more than forty-five minutes on the Directed Writing. Some candidates prefer to start off with the translation, to 'get it out the way', but generally speaking it is probably better to leave the translation until after you have finished the questions, as you are likely to have a deeper understanding of the text by then, and will find that a help with the translation. The translation is a short passage, broken into five chunks for marking, and you can get a mark out of two for each chunk.

Just as at Standard Grade or Intermediate 2, you do not have to understand all of the text thoroughly: you have to get the gist of the text, and then identify carefully where the answers you need are, taking more time with these areas of the text. Reading is a skill, and a skill you need to work on to allow you to give of your best in the final exam. You are not expected to give every detail, or translate word for word what is in the French text. Sometimes the details will matter, but what is more important is that you demonstrate you have understood what the text is about, and put your answers into good English. If your answers do not make sense, then you can assume they are wrong! You do not have to answer in sentences, but be careful not to give too short answers.

There is a sequence you should follow:

1. Read the information in English about the text at the start: this should give you a clue as to what the answers are going to be about. Now look quickly at the questions: these should give you further clues as to what the passage is about, and help you when you skim it for the first time. Notice also that just above the questions you will find a glossary of words, which will save you having to look up these words in a dictionary.

2. Only now should you look at the text: skim through it to get an idea of what it is about, without using a dictionary. This is a challenging task, as you will want to look up words all the time, but resist the temptation for the first run through.

3. Now go back to the questions, and start looking for where the answers are in the passage. Remember that the questions follow the same order as the text, so you should not have to jump around all over the place. There will also be line refences at the start of each question to help you know where to look. Use a highlighter pen, or underline the chunks of text you think are relevant. Remember to check how many marks each question is worth, as a clue to how much to put in your answers!

4. This is when your dictionary will come into play. But be very careful: it is easy to look up far too many words and end up with not enough time to finish the paper. Get into a pattern when trying to understand a piece of text:

    a) Identify the verbs in the sentence, and look these words up if you do not know them (watch for irregular endings!).

    b) Identify the subjects of the verbs: these might be pronouns, so check who they are referring back to, or nouns, in which case make sure you know what these mean.

    c) Once you have the subjects and verbs, the sentences should make more sense, and it is easier to work out what else you need to know.

Sample Reading paper

Let us look at a past Higher Reading paper, and see how this will work in practice. We will give you the passage, and the questions, but provide some guidance on how to answer: try to answer the questions, and then check your answers against the marking scheme provided by SQA. We will start off with the questions, to set the scene. The translation will be a short passage from the text; leave this until you have answered the questions.

In this article you will read about how French attitudes to holidays have changed. Read the article carefully, then answer in English the questions that follow it.

1. This article describes how French people's attitudes to holidays have changed. They have changed where they choose to go (lines 6–16).

    (a) How has their choice of destination changed?

    (b) Why have they made this change?

    (c) Why has Brittany become even more popular?

2. Holiday activities have also changed (lines 17–26).

    (a) Which kinds of activities are no longer popular?

    (b) What do holidaymakers now prefer to do?

    (c) Why have these changes happened?

3. Fashionable holidaymakers have also changed their style of dress (lines 27–36).

    (a) How has women's dress changed?

    (b) What are the main features of men's holiday wear?

4. How has the attitude to sunbathing changed?

5. In the last paragraph (lines 41–42) the writer wonders why these changes have taken place. Give **two** of the reasons he suggests.

This article describes how French people's attitudes to holidays have changed.

Le Français en vacances: ce qui a changé

Sur les bords de la Méditerranée, à Saint-Tropez ou ailleurs, le vacancier arrive. Il a des sandales aux pieds et il marche sur les sables chauds des plages surpeuplées. <u>Comme l'année dernière et les années précédentes, il a réservé des chambres dans un bel hôtel pas trop loin de la plage. Les enfants vont jouer dans la mer pendant que maman passe la journée à se bronzer et que papa boit du vin avec le voisin.</u>　　　　5

Les destinations ont changé

Voilà l'image du passé. Maintenant le vacancier ne se lance plus vers le sud, le sable et la chaleur. Il cherche plutôt la campagne, la randonnée et les gîtes ruraux. La France est devenue, aux yeux des vacanciers, un patchwork magique de petits chemins et de paysages fleuris. Beaucoup préfèrent choisir maintenant les bords de rivière ou les petits villages silencieux loin des grandes routes au lieu des plages bondées de corps très　　10
bronzés.

Il ne faudrait pas croire cependant que les vacanciers ont déserté la côte française. Il y a toujours des centaines de milliers qui se ruent* dans les stations balnéaires. Mais le Français est aujourd'hui un peu plus exigeant: il veut que l'eau de mer soit claire et pas polluée. D'où la popularité de plus en plus marquée de la Bretagne. Elle est devenue la　　15
deuxième destination française des Français après la Côte d'Azur.

Les loisirs ont changé

En plus, les loisirs des Français ont changé en même temps que leurs destinations. Ils ne veulent plus les sports violents comme le squash, le jogging et autres tortures qui font du mal partout. Les nouveaux vacanciers redécouvrent les plaisirs beaucoup plus paisibles de la marche à pied, excellente recette pour le maintien de la forme et la prévention des　　20
accidents cardiovasculaires. Ils continuent à aimer faire du vélo.

Sur les plages, hors-bord* et autres scooters des mers ne sont plus populaires. Ils sont trop bruyants, trop pollueurs pour ne pas dire trop dangereux pour le vacancier qui cherche le calme. Le nouveau passe-temps, c'est de construire et de peindre son propre bateau.

Très en vogue aussi, tous les articles et les vêtements des vacances à la campagne. Les tentes,　　25
sacs à dos, sacs de couchage, thermos, blousons confortables aux couleurs camouflage.

La mode a changé

La mode aussi a subi des changements. Finis les transistors et les maillots de bain fluorescents. Sur la plage, la femme à la mode porte cet été une tenue moins frappante, toujours bleue. Ses vêtements se sont féminisés. Elle se promène avec un sac en paille sur l'épaule et, sur le nez, elle a posé des lunettes avec montures interchangeables qu'elle　　30
peut assortir à son tee-shirt.

continued ➤

Son compagnon est lui aussi devenu plus sobre. Maintenant, il porte des vêtements en fibres naturelles, et il aime le style sportif américain, avec des tee-shirts XXL, extra-extra-larges, qui laissent une impression de liberté. Seule fantaisie: une bandana à la corsaire sur la tête. S'il porte des lunettes, elles sont rondes à la Lennon, noires ou en écaille. 35
Mais surtout pas (quelle horreur!) colorées.

La façon de se bronzer a changé
Et puis, si on veut vraiment bronzer, il faut le faire intelligemment, en bougeant et non pas bêtement étendu sur son drap de bain. Toujours très en vogue: le frisbee et le badminton. Tout nouveau, en revanche: le scatch, un jeu tout simple qui consiste à envoyer une balle que le partenaire rattrape avec un petit disque couvert de Velcro. 40

Pourquoi le vacancier français a-t-il fait tous ces changements? Alors il y a un peu de tout. L'amour de son pays, le désir d'être plus écologiste, la recherche d'un nouvel art de vivre.

Glossary
se ruer (dans)	to dash (into)
un hors-bord	speedboat

This article describes how French people's attitudes to holidays have changed.

1. They have changed where they choose to go (lines 6–16).

   (a) How has their choice of destination changed? **2**

   . . . .

   . . . .

   Two marks, so two things: you are told where to look, and you can then find in the passage that le vacancier ne se lance plus – *subject and verb mean the holidaymaker no longer dashes (watch that reflexive verb!) – towards the south, sun and heat. The passage then goes on* il cherche, *that is, he looks for . . .*

   (b) Why have they made this change? **2**

   . . . .

   . . . .

   The magic word to look for is préfèrent, *as this is the value judgement: you need two marks, so what do they prefer to what?*

   (c) Why has Brittany become even more popular? **1**

   . . . .

   . . . .

   You can find popularité *and* la Bretagne *easily. A little trick here:* D'où *means 'that is why', so the answer is just before this.*

2. Holiday activities have also changed (lines 17–26).

   (a) Which kinds of activities are no longer popular? **2**

   . . . .

   . . . .

   Make sure you get all the details here, so one mark is for the 'violent sports': detail them, and the other mark is for sur les plages, *with details again. If in doubt when answering a question, give details, as long as you are sure they are correct.*

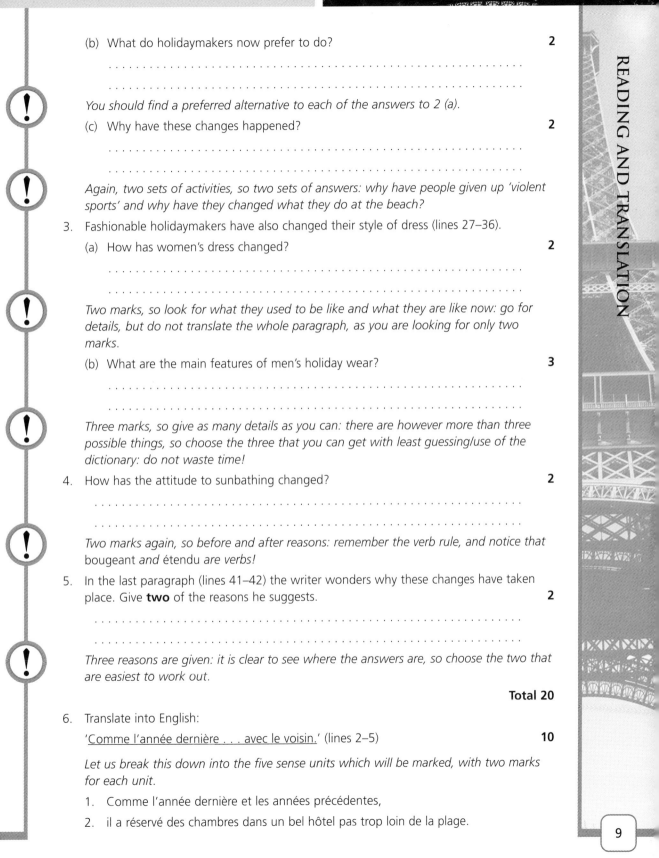

(b) What do holidaymakers now prefer to do? 2

. . . .

. . . .

You should find a preferred alternative to each of the answers to 2 (a).

(c) Why have these changes happened? 2

. . . .

. . . .

Again, two sets of activities, so two sets of answers: why have people given up 'violent sports' and why have they changed what they do at the beach?

3. Fashionable holidaymakers have also changed their style of dress (lines 27–36).

    (a) How has women's dress changed? 2

    . . . .

    . . . .

    Two marks, so look for what they used to be like and what they are like now: go for details, but do not translate the whole paragraph, as you are looking for only two marks.

    (b) What are the main features of men's holiday wear? 3

    . . . .

    . . . .

    Three marks, so give as many details as you can: there are however more than three possible things, so choose the three that you can get with least guessing/use of the dictionary: do not waste time!

4. How has the attitude to sunbathing changed? 2

    . . . .

    . . . .

    Two marks again, so before and after reasons: remember the verb rule, and notice that bougeant *and* étendu *are verbs!*

5. In the last paragraph (lines 41–42) the writer wonders why these changes have taken place. Give **two** of the reasons he suggests. 2

    . . . .

    . . . .

    Three reasons are given: it is clear to see where the answers are, so choose the two that are easiest to work out.

Total 20

6. Translate into English:

    'Comme l'année dernière . . . avec le voisin.' (lines 2–5) 10

    Let us break this down into the five sense units which will be marked, with two marks for each unit.

    1. Comme l'année dernière et les années précédentes,

    2. il a réservé des chambres dans un bel hôtel pas trop loin de la plage.

3. Les enfants vont jouer dans la mer

4. pendant que maman passe la journée à se bronzer

5. et que papa boit du vin avec le voisin.

Unlike the reading questions, it is important that you get every detail here, and that you transmit the message the author was giving in French. Make sure you get the verb tenses right!

For the first unit, make sure you get the correct translation of comme, *one which makes sense, and remember to put the adjectives in front of the nouns.*

For the second unit, make sure you put in every word, apart from des, *which we can do without in English.*

In the third unit, the trick is to get the correct tense of the verb.

In the fourth unit, watch out for the reflexive verb when using a dictionary.

The last unit has a couple of words in it which we do not need in English, and would make the translation wrong if we included them.

Now try to translate the passage, and then check your answer against the marking scheme.

Marking scheme

1. This article describes how French people's attitudes to holidays have changed. They have changed where they choose to go (lines 6–16).

   (a) How has their choice of destination changed?   **2**
   - —   no longer rushing to sun and sand
   - —   instead choosing the countryside

   (b) Why have they made this change?   **2**
   - —   prefer peace and quiet
   - —   to <u>crowded</u> beaches

   (c) Why has Brittany become even more popular?   **1**
   - —   the water is clear/unpolluted

2. Holiday activities have also changed (lines 17–26).

   (a) Which kinds of activities are no longer popular?   **2**
   - —   violent/strenuous sports (**or** list)
   - —   noisy/polluting/dangerous activities (**or** examples)

   (b) What do holidaymakers now prefer to do?   **2**
   - —   gentle sports (**or** examples)
   - —   building/painting one's own boat

   (c) Why have these changes happened?   **2**
   - —   strenuous sports make you ache/gentle sports are good for you/your heart
   - —   speedboats, etc. are noisy/dangerous

   If the reasons required for the answer to (c) are contained in the answers to (a) and (b) **instead**, give the points in (a) and (b).

3. Fashionable holidaymakers have also changed their style of dress (lines 27–36).

    (a) How has women's dress changed? **2**

    — softer colours/blue/less striking

    — (more) feminine

    (b) What are the main features of men's holiday wear? **3**

    — less colourful

    — natural fibres

    — (very) loose-fitting

    — headband/bandanna

    — John Lennon (sun) glasses/small, round glasses

4. How has the attitude to sunbathing changed? **2**

    — don't just lie (on the beach)

    — move about/do some activity/sport (**or** name sports)

5. In the last paragraph (lines 41–42) the writer wonders why these changes have taken place. Give **two** of the reasons he suggests. **2**

    — love of their country

    — awareness of environmental issues

    — looking for a new style of life.

Total 20

6. Translation sense units:

    1. Like last year and the preceding years,

    2. he has reserved rooms in a fine hotel not too far from the beach.

    3. The children will play in the sea

    4. while mum spends the day sunbathing

    5. and dad drinks wine with the neighbour.

    Each sense unit to be awarded 2, 1 or 0 marks, according to the descriptions of performance in Translation provided in the Arrangements Document. **10**

UNIT AND COURSE READING QUESTIONS

Unit Reading

You would normally be expected to complete these Reading assessments in a time of 55–75 minutes. You are allowed a dictionary. You do not have to translate any of the text, and you do not need to answer in sentences. However, make sure your answers give enough details.

This article describes how French people use the Internet to find partners.

La vogue des rencontres sur Internet

Près de 4 millions de Français fréquentent chaque jour les sites de rencontres sur Internet. Hommes, femmes, jeunes et moins jeunes: tous espèrent y trouver l'amour …

Il est 21 heures. Léo, 4 ans, et Élisa, 8 ans, sont couchés. Leur maman peut souffler. 'Je mange un petit quelque chose et je commence.' Deux fois par semaine, le mardi et le vendredi, Patricia, 32 ans, prof de maths dans un collège de Nantes, devient *La Reine des Fées* …   5

Jusqu'à minuit, elle part à la rencontre d'inconnus avec qui elle papote,* parle, échange des messages …

12 millions de célibataires

Patricia fait partie de ces millions de Français qui se connectent chaque jour sur un des nombreux sites de rencontres sur Internet. Ces sites s'appellent Meetic, Net Club, Match, Se rencontrer …   10

Leur objectif: mettre en contact les personnes seules, leur permettre de communiquer en direct par messages.

Et le marché est immense: la France compte environ 12 millions de célibataires. Un Français sur cinq vit seul! Et tous ces gens rêvent de soirées qui ressemblent à autre chose qu'un tête-à-tête avec la télé.   15

continued ➤

Rencontrer l'amour sur Internet. La dernière mode en date pour les branchés* des grandes villes?

Ce n'est pas une mode. C'est un phénomène de société, un changement dans le comportement des solitaires. Ce qui était inconcevable il y a dix ans est en train de devenir le premier mode de rencontre, avant le travail ou les soirées entre amis.   20

'Pas le temps de sortir … '

Patricia a découvert le site de rencontres Match en janvier dernier: 'Je sortais très malheureuse d'un divorce difficile, persuadée que je ne trouverais jamais le bonheur. Entre mon travail de professeur et mes deux enfants, je n'ai pas le temps de sortir, encore moins de rencontrer des amis nouveaux.'

Une collègue lui confie avoir rencontré son mari sur Internet. 'D'abord j'ai trouvé ça   25 ridicule.'

Mais quelques jours plus tard elle regarde le site elle-même. 'Comme c'était gratuit, je me suis inscrite. J'ai rempli ma fiche signalétique* et le lendemain des hommes m'ont proposé de dialoguer avec eux.'

La Reine des Fées

Tout nouvel inscrit sur un site de rencontres doit choisir un pseudonyme et remplir une   30 'fiche'. On y apprend que Patricia, alias *La Reine des Fées*, a les yeux couleur noisette, les cheveux blonds coupés court, deux enfants, un penchant pour les restaurants italiens et les films à suspense, déteste les hommes arrogants, pratique la randonnée … et rêve encore de rencontrer le grand amour.

Glossary

papoter	to chat
branché	up-to-the minute or trendy person
fiche signalétique	personal information form

This article describes how French people use the Internet to find partners.

1. Patricia has started to use the Internet to meet people (lines 4–9).

    (a) When does she do this? Give details.   **4**

    . . . .

    . . . .

    . . . .

    (b) Who does she chat to?   **1**

    . . . .

2. We are told who goes on to the chat sites (lines 10–17).

   (a) What kind of people are most attracted? **1**

   . . . .

   (b) What do they hope to do? **2**

   . . . .

   . . . .

   (c) Why have so many people started to go on to this kind of site? **2**

   . . . .

   . . . .

3. The author suggests this may just be for very fashionable people (lines 18–20).

   (a) Does he agree? Give a reason for your answer. **1**

   . . . .

   (b) What were the usual ways of meeting people? **2**

   . . . .

   . . . .

4. Patricia explains how she got started with online chatting (lines 21–29).

   (a) How did she first hear about it? **2**

   . . . .

   . . . .

   (b) What did she think of the idea at first? **1**

   . . . .

   (c) Why did she sign up in the end? **1**

   . . . .

5. In the last paragraph (lines 30–34) we find out more about Patricia.

   (a) What does she look like? Give details. **2**

   . . . .

   . . . .

   (b) What is she looking for? **1**

   . . . .

   Total 20

This article gives French parents advice on what happens if their child is asked to repeat a year.

Scolarité: le redoublement est-il un échec?

Interview avec Valérie Sultan, professeur principal en classe de troisième

Dans quelle mesure un redoublement peut-il être positif?

Un redoublement n'est pas forcément synonyme d'échec. Au contraire, il peut permettre à l'enfant de repartir sur des bases nouvelles.

Mais faire redoubler un élève, c'est toujours un pari. Le redoublement peut être une chance pour l'élève qui a connu un drame dans sa vie (un mort dans la famille, par exemple) et pour celui qui a un niveau scolaire un peu juste mais fait néanmoins des efforts pour avoir de meilleurs résultats.   5

Je pense par exemple à un enfant de sixième qui éprouve des difficultés à s'adapter à l'enseignement du collège, ou à un adolescent qui, en pleine transformation physique et psychologique, est préoccupé par autre chose que l'école et a besoin de respirer quelques mois.   10

Mais il est important de se souvenir du fait que, pour que le redoublement soit une chance, il ne faut pas le présenter comme une punition.

Faut-il faire le forcing pour faire passer son enfant dans la classe supérieure?*

Il est toujours préférable de discuter d'abord avec l'école. Conseillers d'orientation et professeurs travaillent tous dans l'intérêt de l'élève. Lorsqu'on est parent, on a une relation intime avec son enfant. Du coup, on ne voit pas forcément la réalité, et on peut   15
se tromper. Les enseignants peuvent avoir davantage de distance.

Les idées des parents

Lors des rencontres parents–professeurs, nous sommes ainsi capables de repérer que le désir de l'un n'est pas forcément celui de l'autre: par exemple, les parents veulent absolument que leur enfant fasse une seconde générale avec l'intention de préparer le bac scientifique, alors que l'élève a un autre projet en tête.   20

Y a-t-il des classes où il est préférable de ne pas contester le redoublement?

Oui, ce sont les classes 'importantes': la sixième et la quatrième, au cours de laquelle les élèves apprennent une seconde langue vivante.

continued ➤

Quant à la troisième, après avoir évalué le niveau des élèves à la fin de leur temps en collège, nous ne retenons le redoublement que pour une petite partie d'entre eux. On propose que les autres adolescents en difficulté sont orientés vers un lycée professionnel. 25

Dans les classes de sixième, quatrième et troisième, ce sont tous les professeurs de la classe qui décident de faire passer ou redoubler l'enfant. Si la famille veut contester son choix, elle est obligée de faire appel.

En cinquième, c'est différent: les professeurs donnent des conseils sur l'orientation. C'est la famille qui prend la décision finale. 30

Glossary

faire le forcing   put on pressure

This article gives French parents advice on what happens if their child is asked to repeat a year.

1. Mme Sultan talks about how repeating a year is always a gamble (lines 1–12).

    (a) When might it be a good opportunity for a pupil? Give two examples.   **2**

        . . . .

        . . . .

    (b) She mentions two further cases where it could be advisable. Give details.   **2**

        . . . .

        . . . .

    (c) What is it important to bear in mind?   **1**

        . . . .

2. We are told about the danger of putting too much pressure on the pupil (lines 13–16).

    (a) What should parents do?   **1**

        . . . .

    (b) Why should they do this?   **2**

        . . . .

        . . . .

3. Mme Sultan suggests that parents do not always see things correctly (lines 17–20).

    (a) When does she notice this?   **1**

        . . . .

    (b) What do teachers often notice?   **2**

        . . . .

        . . . .

4. In some classes parents should just accept that their child should repeat the year, according to Mme Sultan (lines 21–30).

    (a) Why should parents accept this in *sixième* (first year) and *quatrième* (third year)?   **2**

    . . . .

    . . . .

    (b) Why do very few pupils repeat *troisième* (fourth year)?   **2**

    . . . .

    . . . .

    (c) What is different about the situation in *cinquième* (second year)?   **1**

    . . . .

Total 16

Course Reading

You would normally be expected to complete these Reading assessments in a time of about 60 minutes each. You are allowed a dictionary. You do not need to answer in sentences. However, make sure your answers give enough details.

These assessments include a translation task; you will find guidance on tackling translation in Chapter 5.

This article describes how important fashion is to sports clothes in France.

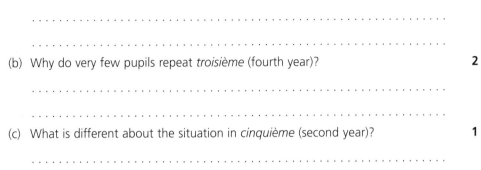

La mode du sport: les baskets et les jogging!

On est en 1986. Les dirigeants de la marque aux trois bandes signent avec Run DMC le premier contrat non-sportif de l'histoire du sport: un million de dollars. Dans un seul week-end, il se vend pour 22 millions de dollars de produits siglés Adidas–Run DMC. Aujourd'hui, 79% des jeunes Français de 8 à 19 ans, quand ils pensent à des marques de vêtements, citent des griffes de sport. Stella McCartney fait un malheur* chez Adidas   5
depuis qu'elle y dessine une collection. Une génération d'urbains adeptes du «cool» se retrouve dans les modèles de Puma, qui collabore avec Philippe Starck ou Alexander McQueen.

continued ➤

Les trois grandes marques, Nike, Adidas et Puma, sont en train de quitter le sport pour la mode. <u>Jusqu'à présent, pour les marques de sport, toute leur énergie était consacrée à la 10 technologie et la performance. Les femmes, qui ne représentent que 30% de la clientèle, constituent «le» marché de demain. Avant, on prenait les vêtements pour hommes, on les taillait plus courts et plus étroits et voilà, c'était la ligne féminine.</u>

Un responsable du style chez Nike à Portland (Oregon, Etats-Unis) peut-il séduire une consommatrice parisienne devouée à la mode? Pas vraiment. Les Américains pensent 15 encore que les filles, c'est du rose et blanc porté assez large, quand les Londoniennes ou Parisiennes ont adopté jeans serré et look rock. Les dirigeants de Nike ont pris en compte l'existence du consommateur mode. Conséquence: on a recruté en Europe des dénicheurs de tendances dont la mission est d'envoyer à Portland des comptes rendus réguliers sur l'évolution des modes dans la rue. On va s'orienter vers la mode, oui, et vers les femmes, 20 c'est certain, mais avec des stylistes maison. Après tout, l'entreprise au swoosh est l'une des plus grandes employeuses de designers au monde.

Contrairement aux Allemandes (des sportives sérieuses) ou aux Britanniques (des fanatiques de running), les Françaises sont avant tout folles de style. À elles les collections de Stella McCartney, petits hauts* couleur taupe et bas de jogging serrés. Les gens 25 d'Adidas ont fait le même calcul que ceux de Nike: les femmes! Et pour les conquérir il faut insister sur le côté mode et style, à la différence des acheteurs hommes, qui sont encore centrés sur le sport.

La collaboration de Stella McCartney avec la marque est née un jour de 2000 lors d'une table ronde réunissant, autour des collaborateurs d'Adidas, des créateurs venus parler 30 style. Et Stella, qui est une sportive (natation, yoga), a pu dire: *«Pourquoi est-on obligées de ressembler à des sacs?»* Depuis, elle et ses collaborateurs londoniens travaillent avec le bureau de style d'Adidas, en Allemagne.

Quant à Puma, quoi alors? Voilà la description de l'acheteur type Puma: *«Ce n'est pas forcément le mec le plus beau, le meilleur, mais c'est le plus cool, et sa copine est la* 35 *mieux.»* Car, avec des bureaux de style à Londres, Boston et à Herzogenaurach, plus de 100 personnes en tout, sans compter une cellule «sport fashion» d'une cinquantaine de designers à Londres, Puma se trouve branché. *«Les coupes sont près du corps, les matières légères, les shorts descendent aux genoux, même nos étiquettes sont rigolotes.»*

Qui inventera l'équivalent du sweat à capuche du XXIe siècle? Une chose est certaine: les 40 marques de sport font la jonction entre les différents styles et looks de la rue. Le vintage, toujours; les sports *«porteurs d'image»* (surf, skate) bien sûr; et les collections femmes, évidemment. Dans le textile, les hauts se vendent mieux que les bas, car le jeans joue désormais le rôle du casual. Le jackpot reviendra à la marque qui inventera de quoi habiller les femmes en bas. Trois, deux, un, partez! 45

Glossary

faire un malheur	be a smash hit, great success
un haut	a top (article of clothing)

This article describes how important fashion is to sports clothes in France.

1. In the first paragraph, we are given some background information (lines 1–8).

    (a) Why are the rap group Run DMC mentioned?   2

    . . . .

    . . . .

    (b) What statistic are we given about young French people?   2

    . . . .

    (c) Why is Stella McCartney mentioned?   1

    . . . .

2. We are told in paragraph 3 (lines 14–22) how Nike is dealing with the issue.

    (a) How do young American and young French girls differ in their approach to
        fashion?   2

    . . . .

    . . . .

    (b) What are Nike doing about this?   2

    . . . .

    . . . .

3. In paragraphs 4 and 5 (lines 23–33), the author talks about Adidas.

    (a) What Adidas products do young French girls like?   2

    . . . .

    . . . .

    (b) What differences between male and female customers are noticed?   2

    . . . .

    . . . .

    (c) How did Stella McCartney come to work with Adidas? Give details.   3

    . . . .

    . . . .

    . . . .

4. In paragraph 6 we are told about Puma's involvement in sports fashion (lines 34–39).

    (a) How do Puma describe their average male customer?   3

    . . . .

    . . . .

    . . . .

(b) What do they say about their clothes? Mention any three things.   **3**

. . . .

. . . .

. . . .

5. In paragraph 7 the author looks to the future (lines 40–45).

(a) What question does the author ask?   **1**

. . . .

(b) Why do sports tops sell better than sports trousers?   **1**

. . . .

Total 24

Translate 'Jusqu'à présent … la ligne féminine.' (lines 10 to 13).   **10**

**This article describes how
texting is becoming more used
in France.**

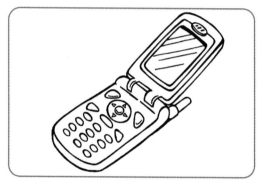

SMS, textos: dites 'Je t'M' avec le pouce!

**En quelques années, les mini-messages ou SMS ont conquis tous les propriétaires
de mobile! À tel point que le pouce est devenu un organe de communication à
part entière. Qui aujourd'hui envoie encore une lettre d'amour par la poste pour
la Saint-Valentin? Un message texte suffit!**

Plus de 72% des gens possèdent un téléphone portable en Europe. Et les SMS sont   5
devenus une partie essentielle de cette révolution numérique. En Angleterre, plus d'un
milliard de messages sont envoyés par mois. En France, ce sont 35 millions de vœux
électroniques qui ont été échangés le premier janvier 2006.

Qui sont les 'texters'?

Mais qui sont les agités du pouce? Si tout le monde envoie des messages de temps en
temps, les véritables adeptes, qui privilégient ce moyen de communication, sont   10
essentiellement les plus jeunes. 90% des ados préféreraient envoyer des messages que
de parler de vive voix au téléphone. Et les jeunes adultes ne sont pas en reste: 78% des
Français de 18–24 ans sont des habitués des SMS. Les femmes seraient un peu plus
textos que les hommes, mais on ne peut guère parler de la féminisation du pouce: les

continued ➤

hommes s'en servent chaque jour aussi! Les utilisations majoritaires seraient les messages 15
d'amour, l'amitié et autres fonctions plutôt relationnelles et sociales. Le développement
des textos est tel que certains spécialistes n'hésitent pas à parler d'addiction, et des
cliniques proposent même des cures de désintoxication.

Un monde à part

Mais surtout aujourd'hui les messages textes sont devenus un moyen à part entière de
contacter son réseau de proches. Et cela s'adresse pratiquement exclusivement au cercle 20
d'amis: une étude anglaise a montré que les 'texters' n'envoient pas des SMS
indifféremment à tout leur carnet d'adresse. Ils envoient de manière intensive des textos
à un petit groupe d'amis. Les SMS sont envoyés moins facilement à un membre de la
famille. À noter que de nouvelles fonctionnalités, tel que l'accès aux logiciels de messagerie
instantanée du web sur son mobile, devraient renforcer ce phénomène. 25

Le pouce des timides

Certains spécialistes pensent que les textos sont, encore plus que les forums de
discussions, la bouée de sauvetage des grands timides et des phobiques sociaux. En clair,
tous ceux qui ont du mal à s'exprimer en face à face. Ces véritables 'handicapés sociaux'
en sont réduits à même éviter la conversation téléphonique pour lui préférer le message
texte. Des scientifiques ont montré que les personnes qui ont tendance à nouer des 30
amitiés plutôt dans le monde virtuel de l'Internet sont aussi plus attirées par les messages
textes. Les SMS seraient même utilisés par certains à la manière d'un 'chat'. Avec
l'avantage pour les timides d'avoir plus de temps pour réfléchir à ses réponses.

Y a klk1?

Si le SMS est devenu un mode de communication à part entière, il a aussi son langage …
qui d'ailleurs hérisse le poil* des puristes. Écriture phonétique, lettres qui remplacent des 35
syllabes … Pour les plus âgés, cela ne ressemble à rien. Celui-ci renforce encore plus le
sentiment d'appartenance à un groupe, avec son langage et ses codes. Mais ses
détracteurs soulignent que cette simplification limite la richesse de la discussion. Il est
difficile en effet de philosopher en langage SMS … On notera néanmoins des initiatives
intéressantes, telles que les fables de La Fontaine en SMS publiées par Phil Marso. 40
Même si vous êtes un adepte des SMS, n'oubliez pas tout de même de rencontrer vos
amis dans la vraie vie. Et alors éteignez votre portable!

Glossary

hérisser le poil (de)   annoy

This article describes how texting is becoming more used in France.

1. In the first paragraph, we are given some information about the growth of texting in
    Europe (lines 5–8).

    (a) What three statistics are we given?   **3**

    . . . .

    . . . .

    . . . .

2. We are told in paragraph 2 (lines 9–18) who is using texting.

    (a) Which group of people use texts most?   **1**

    . . . .

    (b) What are we told about the relative use by men and women?   **2**

    . . . .

    . . . .

    (c) What are the main reasons for using texts?   **3**

    . . . .

    . . . .

    . . . .

3. In paragraph 3 (lines 19–25), the author talks about who is texted.

    (a) Who are the main recipients of text messages?   **1**

    . . . .

    (b) Who is less likely to receive a text?   **1**

    . . . .

    (c) What is likely to increase text use in the future?   **1**

    . . . .

4. In paragraph 4 we are told more about texters (lines 26–33).

    (a) Who is texting really useful for?   **2**

    . . . .

    . . . .

    (b) What do they prefer?   **1**

    . . . .

    (c) How do Internet users use texting and what advantage does this have for them?   **2**

    . . . .

    . . . .

5. In paragraph 5 the author looks at text language (lines 34–42).

    (a) Who has difficulty with text language?   **1**

    . . . .

    (b) What advantages and disadvantages does text language have? Give details.   **4**

    . . . .

    . . . .

    . . . .

    . . . .

(c)   What final piece of advice does the author give?   **2**

. . . .

. . . .

Total 24

Translate 'En quelques années … suffit!' (lines 1 to 4).   **10**

ANSWERS TO THE READING QUESTIONS

La vogue des rencontres sur Internet

This article describes how French people use the Internet to find partners.

1. Patricia has started to use the Internet to meet people (lines 4–9).
   - (a) When does she do this? Give details.   **4**
     - — when her children are in bed
     - — twice a week
     - — Tuesdays and Fridays
     - — from 9 until midnight
   - (b) Who does she chat to?   **1**
     - — strangers

2. We are told who goes on to the chat sites (lines 10–17).
   - (a) What kind of people are most attracted?   **1**
     - — single or unmarried people
   - (b) What do they hope to do?   **2**
     - — get in touch with other single people
     - — be able to send messages
   - (c) Why have so many people started to go on to this kind of site?   **2**
     - — there are 12 million single people in France
     - — one person in five lives alone
     - — they don't want to just talk to the television (**any two**)

3. The author suggests this may just be for very fashionable people (lines 18–20)
   - (a) Does he agree? Give a reason for your answer.   **1**
     - — No: he says it is not a fashion/it is a change in behaviour
   - (b) What were the usual ways of meeting people?   **2**
     - — at work
     - — or evenings out with friends

4. Patricia explains how she got started with online chatting (lines 21–29).
   - (a) How did she first hear about it?   **2**
     - — a colleague told her
     - — she had met her husband online
   - (b) What did she think of the idea at first?   **1**
     - — it was ridiculous

(c) Why did she sign up in the end? **1**

— it was free

5. In the last paragraph (lines 30–34) we find out more about Patricia.

(a) What does she look like? Give details. **2**

— hazel eyes

— short blond hair

(b) What is she looking for? **1**

— the love of her life

Scolarité: le redoublement est-il un échec?

This article gives French parents advice on what happens if their child is asked to repeat a year.

1. Mme Sultan talks about how repeating a year is always a gamble (lines 1–12).

(a) When might it be a good opportunity for a pupil? Give two examples. **2**

— when there has been a family drama (such as a death)

— when someone is not quite making the grade but is trying hard

(b) She mentions two further cases where it could be advisable. Give details. **2**

— a first-year pupil who is not adjusting well to the new school

— an adolescent whose mind is elsewhere **or** an adolescent who needs breathing space

(c) What is it important to bear in mind? **1**

— it must not be presented as a punishment

2. We are told about the danger of putting too much pressure on the pupil (lines 13–16).

(a) What should parents do? **1**

— speak to the school first

(b) Why should they do this? **2**

— they are often too close to the child to see things clearly

— teachers can be more objective

— teachers and guidance staff work in the interests of the child (**any two**)

3. Mme Sultan suggests that parents do not always see things correctly (lines 17–20).

(a) When does she notice this? **1**

— at parents' nights/meetings

(b) What do teachers often notice? **2**

— that the parents want one thing

— and the pupil has other ideas

4. In some classes parents should just accept that their child should repeat the year, according to Mme Sultan (lines 21–30).

    (a) Why should parents accept this in *sixième* (first year) and *quatrième* (third year)?   **2**
        — these are important years
        — where the pupils are learning a new language

    (b) Why do very few pupils repeat *troisième* (fourth year)?   **2**
        — the pupils' work is evaluated
        — most pupils in difficulty are recommended to go to a technical school

    (c) What is different about the situation in *cinquième* (second year)?   **1**
        — here it is the family who decides whether the pupil should repeat
        or
        — in the other years, the teachers decide

La mode du sport: les baskets et les jogging!

This article describes how important fashion is to sports clothes in France.

1. In the first paragraph, we are given some background information (lines 1–8).

    (a) Why are the rap group Run DMC mentioned?   **2**
        — they were the first people to sign a contract with Adidas (sports clothing manufacturer)
        — who were not sport stars
        or
        — in a single weekend they sold
        — 22 million dollars worth of Adidas–Run DMC clothing

    (b) What statistic are we given about young French people?   **2**
        — 79% of young people (8–19-year-olds)
        — think of sports brands when they think of clothes

    (c) Why is Stella McCartney mentioned?   **1**
        — she has had a lot of success with a collection for Adidas

2. We are told in paragraph 3 (lines 14–22) how Nike is dealing with the issue.

    (a) How do young American and young French girls differ in their approach to fashion?   **2**
        — young American girls still wear loose pink and white clothes
        — young Parisian girls wear tight jeans and rock-style clothes

    (b) What are Nike doing about this?   **2**
        — they have recruited fashion observers
        — who send reports on fashion to Nike (Portland)

3. In paragraphs 4 and 5 (lines 23–33), the author talks about Adidas.
   (a) What Adidas products do young French girls like? **2**
   any two of
   — Stella McCartney collections
   — little taupe-coloured tops
   — close-fitting jogging bottoms (leggings)
   (b) What differences between male and female customers are noticed? **2**
   — women are focused on fashion and style
   — men are still focused on sport
   (c) How did Stella McCartney come to work with Adidas? Give details. **3**
   — they met at a round-table discussion
   — she is interested in sport
   — she asked why people had to look like sacks (bags) in sportswear
4. In paragraph 6 we are told about Puma's involvement in sports fashion (lines 34–39).
   (a) How do Puma describe their average male customer? **3**
   — he's not necessarily the best-looking
   — he is the coolest
   — he has the best girlfriend
   (b) What do they say about their clothes? Mention any three things. **3**
   any three of
   — very fashionable
   — close-fitting
   — light materials
   — knee-length shorts
   — even their labels are fun
5. In paragraph 7 the author looks to the future (lines 40–45).
   (a) What question does the author ask? **1**
   — who will invent the twenty-first century equivalent of the hooded top?
   (b) Why do sports tops sell better than sports trousers? **1**
   — because jeans are the norm for casual wear

Translation
Until now, for sports brands (makers), all their energy was devoted to technology and performance./Women, who represent only 30% of their customers,/make up the market of tomorrow./Previously, they took men's clothes, made them shorter and tighter (narrower),/and there you had the women's line.

10

SMS, textos: dites 'Je t'M' avec le pouce!

This article describes how texting is becoming more used in France.

1. In the first paragraph, we are given some information about the growth of texting in Europe (lines 5–8).

    (a) What three statistics are we given? **3**
    — more than 72% of Europeans own a mobile phone
    — in England more than a *milliard* (billion/thousand million) messages are sent every month
    — on New Year's Day 2006 in France 35 million greetings were exchanged

2. We are told in paragraph 2 (lines 9–18) who is using texting.

    (a) Which group of people use texts most? **1**
    — the very young/adolescents/teenagers

    (b) What are we told about the relative use by men and women? **2**
    — women text a little more
    — but men text every day as well

    (c) What are the main reasons for using texts? **3**
    — love
    — friendship
    — social reasons

3. In paragraph 3 (lines 19–25), the author talks about who is texted.

    (a) Who are the main recipients of text messages? **1**
    — close friends/a circle of friends

    (b) Who is less likely to receive a text? **1**
    — a family member

    (c) What is likely to increase text use in the future? **1**
    — being able to access instant messaging from the Internet

4. In paragraph 4 we are told more about texters (lines 26–33).

    (a) Who is texting really useful for? **2**
    — very shy people
    — people who have difficulty talking face to face

    (b) What do they prefer? **1**
    — they prefer texts to phone conversation

    (c) How do Internet users use texting and what advantage does this have for them? **2**
    — they use it like a chat session
    — they have more time to think about their answers

5. In paragraph 5 the author looks at text language (lines 34–42).

    (a) Who has difficulty with text language? **1**
    — older people

(b) What advantages and disadvantages does text language have? Give details.   **4**

—   makes users feel more part of a group

—   with its own language

—   puts limits on the richness of discussion

—   it is hard to philosophise (talk in depth) in a text

(c) What final piece of advice does the author give?   **2**

—   don't forget to meet your friends in real life

—   and switch off your phone when you do

Translation

In a few years text messages, or SMS, have won over all mobile phone owners./To such an extent that the thumb/has become a means of communication in its own right./Who still sends a love letter by post for Valentine's Day?/A text message will do!

10

TRANSLATION

Introduction

This is the area which will be new to you, as translation only appears from Higher onwards. Normally you will be asked to translate a piece of text of three or so sentences, broken down into five sense units. The translation into English is allocated 10 marks. Each sense unit is worth 2 marks, which will be awarded according to the quality and accuracy of the translation into English. In assessing performance, the descriptions below will be used. Each sense unit will be awarded one of the marks shown.

Category	Mark	Description
Good	2	Essential information and relevant details are understood and conveyed clearly and accurately, with appropriate use of English.
Satisfactory	1	Essential information is understood and conveyed clearly and comprehensibly, although some of the details may be translated in an imprecise or inaccurate manner. The key message is conveyed in spite of inaccuracies and weaknesses in the use of English.
Unsatisfactory	0	The candidate fails to demonstrate sufficient understanding of the essential information and relevant details. Errors may include mistranslation and/or the failure to translate relevant details.

Some people prefer to tackle the translation first, to 'get it out of the way'. However, this is probably a bad idea, as you are more likely to understand the piece you are translating when you have answered the questions and know more of the context. You might also spend a long time on the translation at the start of the exam, and not have enough time to answer all the questions. However, as the translation is worth 10 marks and the questions 20, make sure you leave yourself enough time to do the translation justice! That should mean between five and ten minutes, normally.

Sample marking scheme

Here is part of the marking scheme from the 2005 Higher, to show you how a sense unit is marked. The original text for translation was:

> Encouragés par le succès de cette jeune New-Yorkaise des centaines de 'Mendiants d'Internet' ont créé des sites simplement pour faire appel à la générosité des autres. Chacun a une histoire à raconter qui a pour but d'attirer notre compassion.

The table that follows sets out the first sense unit.

Text	Good 2	Satisfactory 1	Unsatisfactory 0
Encouragés par le succès de cette jeune New-Yorkaise,	Encouraged by the success of this/that young New Yorker/ girl from NY,		
Encouragés	Encouraged		By encouraging To be encouraged Encouragement
par le succès	by the success	through the success	the successes
de cette	of this/that	the	these/those
jeune New-Yorkaise	young New Yorker/ young girl from New York young person/woman/ youngster from New York young inhabitant of New York	youth/teenager New Yorkian	child omission of 'young' (except with 'girl') New Yorkshire New Yorkaise New Yorkers young people from New York

Notice that if you miss out 'young' you lose both marks. Making a mistake between singular and plural also loses you both marks. The translation here should be more or less word for word. However, the last sense unit is different, and the following table sets this out.

Text	Good 2	Satisfactory 1
qui a pour but d'attirer notre compassion.	with the aim of attracting our compassion.	
qui a pour but	that/which aims to whose aim/goal is to which is aimed at the purpose/intention of which is with the aim/objective of	to/in order to
d'attirer	(to) attract/(of) attracting (to) arouse/engage	(to) entice (to) lure (to) incite (to) gain/win (to) appeal to (to) draw
notre compassion	our compassion/sympathy/pity	your

The French literally says 'which has for goal to attract our compassion', which of course makes no sense in English, so we have to change it around to make sense. Getting right what you should leave and what you should change is the hardest part of doing a translation. Practice will make you better at this. Try to translate the rest of the extract: *mendiant* means beggar. The suggested answer is on the next page.

How to get good marks

The rules for understanding the French in order to make a translation are the same as for answering questions: look for the verbs first, find the subjects of these verbs, and the rest should fall into place more easily. There are some differences as well, however. You need to give **all** the details, you must answer in sentences if the original is in sentences, and you have to get things just right. It is no good getting the right verb, for instance, but the wrong tense.

There are some important things to remember:

◆ If what you have written does not make sense in English, then it is guaranteed to be wrong.

◆ Make sure you get the correct tense of the verb.

◆ Do not miss out any adjectives or adverbs: it is easy to forget a little word, and most marks are lost this way.

◆ Missing out one word can lose you both marks for that sense unit: check afterwards that you have got everything, perhaps by striking out the words on the question paper.

◆ You do not have to do a word-for-word translation: just get the sense of the original into English with all the details in place.

Practising translation

Try translating small chunks of text from any passage you read, to get into the habit of translating, and discuss your answers with others. The Course Reading papers in Chapter 3 (pp. 17–22) include translation tasks which you can use for practice, and model translations are given in Chapter 4. Another useful thing to do is to take a piece of French text and run it through a translation machine or site on the Internet such as Babelfish or Google Language Tools. This will give you a translation which will probably be in bad English and will not always make sense. Try to make it make sense in English, looking at the original and coming up with a proper translation. This will develop your attention to detail, and will help you think about the quality of the English in your answer. And remember, if you put your own English text into a translation machine and ask it to translate it into French, the result will probably be in bad French and will not always make sense!

Suggested translation of text

Encouraged by the success of this girl from New York, hundreds of 'Internet Beggars' have created sites simply to appeal to the generosity of others/other people. Each one has a story to tell with the aim of attracting our compassion.

LISTENING

Introduction

Listening is worth **20 per cent** of your final mark. The listening passage will take the form of a dialogue, in which one person is asked and answers questions on a topic. You will be asked questions about the interviewee's answers. The Unit and Course assessments follow the same format, and will be at about the same level of difficulty. However, for the Unit or NAB assessment you will get to hear the dialogue three times, for the Higher exam just twice. The conversation will last two to three minutes, there will be a gap of two minutes, and then you will hear it again.

Practising listening skills

When practising for or actually doing the Unit assessment, make sure that the first time through you simply listen, and do not be tempted to jot down notes, as that may make you miss important information which is following! Just listen and make mental notes as to where you have to concentrate particularly hard the next time. If you can get into this habit, it will help you do the same in the final exam. Many people fear they will have forgotten the answers by the time they come to write them down, but trust your own memory!

You will not be allowed to use a dictionary for the Unit listening, so you need to be prepared for the exam in advance, and make sure you know the basic vocabulary for the theme or topic of the Listening assessment. You should know in advance what this will be, as normally you would carry out this assessment towards the end of your study of the topic in question.

You are, however, allowed a dictionary for the Higher Course listening, and this requires a new skill: note-taking in French. While you should not under any circumstances be looking through a dictionary while the listening is going on, you might want to write down one or two words you hear but are not sure of the meaning of, in order to look them up when writing out your final answers.

Listen extra carefully for details you are required to give in your answer. Just as at Standard Grade, if you are not sure of an answer, do not be afraid to guess, as you will get no marks for a blank, but may for an intelligent guess! Equally, as at Standard Grade, if the answer asks for two things, just give two things! The examiner will only give you marks for the first two things you write down, and you will get no credit for something that is correct later on in the answer, if a wrong answer is given before it. SQA's rules also mean that there is no point in putting down a whole lot of potential answers, hoping to cover all the bases: you will get no marks at all in this case.

How to get good marks

So what do you do when you are sitting the exam? What is the best way to go about it?

In some ways the listening at Higher is easier than at Intermediate or Standard Grade, because you only have to keep your concentration solid for eight or nine minutes, rather than half an hour. Here are some steps to take which should help you do your best:

◆ When you are told to open your paper, do so and read the information at the start setting the scene.

◆ Draw a line down the centre of the page, and write your notes on the left of the page when it is time; you should transfer your final answers to the right of the line at the end, and score out your notes with a single line.

◆ Read all the questions carefully, as this will prepare you for what the dialogue is about.

◆ Look for the question words, such as 'why', 'when', in order to know what information you are looking for.

◆ Make sure you get the basics, such as numbers, times, dates, and all the Standard Grade vocabulary for places, weather, and so on (you will find these in Chapter 14, Structures and vocabulary, for revision).

◆ Keep your concentration going for the whole time: do not try to write out your final answers before the last playing of the CD or tape has finished.

The topic of the Listening assessment and the follow-up writing will be drawn from the areas you have studied in your work on the Language Unit: use the checklist in Appendix One to check how well you think you are prepared for each of these areas.

UNIT AND COURSE LISTENING QUESTIONS

Introduction

The texts on the CD have been recorded twice, with a gap of two minutes between them. Try to stick to this, to give you more practice for the real exam. If you want to practise for a Unit assessment, you should listen a third time.

The Listening assessments are based on the six topics of the Higher French Language Unit, but each one may well cover more than one topic area.

For each of the nine Listening assessments given in this chapter, there is an essay question based on the topic. You should try these and might wish to ask your teacher to mark them. If you do the listening and the follow-up writing, you should take 60 minutes in total.

1 Careers

Yvonne is being interviewed about her plans for the future.

1. What does Yvonne tell you about her work? **3**

   . . . .

   . . . .

2. Give details about where she comes from. **3**

   . . . .

   . . . .

3. What does she tell you about her future plans? **4**

   . . . .

   . . . .

   . . . .

4. What problems does she have with her pupils in Scotland? **2**

   . . . .

   . . . .

5. Why might she stay in Scotland? **1**

   . . . .

6. Why does she think it would be possible to settle in Scotland? **3**

   . . . .

   . . . .

7. What do her parents think of this possibility? **4**

   . . . .

   . . . .

   . . . .

Yvonne parle de ses projets pour l'avenir.
Et vous, quels sont vos projets?
Aimeriez-vous aller à l'université?

Écrivez 120–150 mots pour exprimer vos idées.

2 Holidays and travel

Jacques talks about his experiences of holidays with his family and his friends.

1. What does Jacques tell you about his first holidays away from his parents?   **4**

. . . .

. . . .

. . . .

2. When was his first independent holiday?   **1**

. . . .

3. Where did he go, and what did he do there?   **4**

. . . .

. . . .

. . . .

4. Why did he like this holiday?   **3**

. . . .

. . . .

. . . .

5. What annoyed him about going on holiday with his parents?   **2**

. . . .

. . . .

6. Where does he go on holiday nowadays? Give details.   **3**

. . . .

. . . .

. . . .

7. What does he enjoy doing on holiday now?   **3**

. . . .

. . . .

. . . .

Jacques a parlé de ses vacances.
Et vous, qu'est-ce que vous aimez faire en vacances?
Quelles étaient vos meilleurs vacances?

3 School/college

Marie-Claire talks about her schooldays.

1. What does Marie-Claire say when asked if she liked school?   **3**

    . . . .

    . . . .

    . . . .

2. What was good about her first school?   **3**

    . . . .

    . . . .

3. How were her teachers? Give details.   **3**

    . . . .

    . . . .

    . . . .

4. What problems were there with her second school?   **5**

    . . . .

    . . . .

    . . . .

    . . . .

5. Why did she keep going?   **3**

    . . . .

    . . . .

    . . . .

6. What was good about her second school?   **3**

    . . . .

    . . . .

    . . . .

Marie-Claire parle des écoles où elle est allée.
Et vous, est-ce que vous avez aimé l'école?
Qu'est-ce que vous aimeriez changer dans votre école?

4 Tourism/home area

Éric is talking about growing up in a big town.

1. Where did Éric grow up? Give details.   **3**

. . . .

. . . .

. . . .

2. How did he like this place? Give reasons for your answer.   **4**

. . . .

. . . .

. . . .

3. What was not so good?   **2**

. . . .

. . . .

4. What became a problem when he was older? Give details.   **3**

. . . .

. . . .

. . . .

5. Where does he live now, and why?   **3**

. . . .

. . . .

. . . .

6. What are the advantages and disadvantages of living there?   **4**

. . . .

. . . .

. . . .

7. What is he planning to do this summer?   **1**

. . . .

Éric parle de vivre dans une grande ville.
Et vous, où est-ce que vous habitez?
Ça vous plait?
Est-ce que vous allez rester là?

5   Leisure and healthy living

Francine talks about young people and their attitude to drinking alcohol in France.

1. Does she think young French people drink like young Britons? Why?   **2**

    . . . .

    . . . .

2. How have things changed in French families at mealtimes?   **3**

    . . . .

    . . . .

    . . . .

3. When do young French people drink now?   **3**

    . . . .

    . . . .

    . . . .

4. What has changed for young French people? Give details.   **4**

    . . . .

    . . . .

    . . . .

5. Why do young people not always go to cafés to meet their friends?   **2**

    . . . .

    . . . .

6. Is the situation the same for boys and girls? Explain your answer.   **3**

    . . . .

    . . . .

    . . . .

7. What horrifies her about drinking habits in Britain?   **3**

    . . . .

    . . . .

    . . . .

Francine a parlé des jeunes en France et en Écosse.
Et vous, avez-vous assez de liberté?
Que faites-vous le soir et le week-end?

6 Family, friends, society

Sylvain talks about how he gets on with the other members of his family.

1. What does Sylvain tell you about his family? **4**

. . . .

. . . .

. . . .

2. Why is the situation like this? **2**

. . . .

. . . .

3. What does he feel about it? **2**

. . . .

. . . .

4. When does he see his father? **2**

. . . .

. . . .

5. Why are things arranged the way they are? **3**

. . . .

. . . .

. . . .

6. What does he tell you about his two sets of grandparents? **4**

. . . .

. . . .

. . . .

7. What does he tell you about his sister? **3**

. . . .

. . . .

. . . .

Sylvain parle de sa famille.
Et vous, vous vous entendez bien avec votre famille?
Est-ce que votre famille est importante pour vous?
Préférez-vous sortir et parler avec vos copains?

7 Leisure and healthy living

Vincent is talking about what he does in his spare time.

1. What reasons does Vincent give for liking cycling? **2**

    . . . .

    . . . .

2. Why does he cycle less now than before? **1**

    . . . .

3. What does he say about a normal weekend bike trip? Give details. **3**

    . . . .

    . . . .

    . . . .

4. What does he do afterwards? Give details. **3**

    . . . .

    . . . .

    . . . .

5. What other sport does he take part in? Give details. **3**

    . . . .

    . . . .

    . . . .

6. What does he feel about this? Why? **3**

    . . . .

    . . . .

    . . . .

7. What kind of music does he like? **2**

    . . . .

    . . . .

8. What musical instrument is he learning? **1**

    . . . .

9. What problems does he find with this? **2**

    . . . .

    . . . .

Vincent parle de ses loisirs.
Est-ce que votre temps libre est important pour vous?
La musique, vous la trouvez importante dans votre vie?
Préférez-vous participer au sport?

8   Careers

Yvonne talks about her part-time job.

1.   What does she tell you about her job? Give details.   **3**

   . . . .
   . . . .
   . . . .

2.   Why does she work?   **3**

   . . . .
   . . . .
   . . . .

3.   How does she feel about her part-time job? Give details.   **4**

   . . . .
   . . . .
   . . . .

4.   When does she find problems with her work? Why?   **3**

   . . . .
   . . . .
   . . . .

5.   Why did she not have a part-time job when she was a student in France?   **3**

   . . . .
   . . . .
   . . . .

6.   She did work in France. When, and what did she do?   **2**

   . . . .
   . . . .

7.   Why did she like this job?   **2**

   . . . .
   . . . .

Yvonne parle de son boulot.
Et vous, vous avez un boulot?
Est-ce que vos amis travaillent le soir ou le week-end?
Croyez-vous que c'est un danger pour les études?

Chapter 7

HOW TO PASS HIGHER FRENCH

9   Leisure and healthy living

Vincent talks about the differences between eating in France and in Scotland.

1. What is the main difference Vincent notices about where he is? Give details.   **2**

. . . .

. . . .

2. What does he tell us about breakfast in France and Scotland?   **4**

. . . .

. . . .

. . . .

3. What does he feel about 'a full English breakfast'?   **2**

. . . .

. . . .

4. What does he say about lunch and Scotland? Give details.   **4**

. . . .

. . . .

. . . .

5. Why does he mention school pupils?   **2**

. . . .

. . . .

6. What does he tell you about his own habits in France?   **2**

. . . .

. . . .

7. How does he spend his lunchtime in Scotland?   **2**

. . . .

. . . .

8. What is for him the main difference in restaurants in the two countries?   **2**

. . . .

. . . .

Vincent nous parle de sa façon de manger.
Est-ce que la nourriture est importante pour vous?
Est-ce que vous mangez sain?
Préférez-vous sortir et parler avec vos copains à midi, ou rester à la cantine?

44

ANSWERS TO THE LISTENING QUESTIONS

1 Careers

1. works as an assistant in a school/works in a bar/to meet other (young) people **3**

2. student in Lille/from a small village in Northern France/30 km from Lille/half an hour by train (**any three**) **3**

3. go back to uni (study) in September/two more years/come back to Scotland/become teacher **4**

4. some refuse to speak French/others ask 'why do we have to learn French?' **2**

5. she has a boyfriend: it depends on how it works out **1**

6. Glasgow is quite like Lille/there are cheap flights/so she can keep in touch with her family **3**

7. her mother is not keen (would prefer her to stay in France)/but accepts her wishes/her father is happy/he can come to Scotland and play golf **4**

2 Holidays and travel

1. at the age of 13/went to a *colonie* (holiday camp) with friends/in south of France/it was an organised trip **4**

2. when he was 17 (in last year at school) **1**

3. Britanny (**or** near St Malo)/cycled/camped/went swimming in the sea (**or** every morning) **4**

4. could get up late/didn't have to go sightseeing (old buildings **or** monuments)/could eat when and as they wanted **3**

5. rules for mealtimes/had to get up at eight for breakfast/had to be back for lunch at one (**any two**) **2**

6. with his parents to the south (**or** same house)/with his girlfriend further (**or** by plane)/to Greece or Italy **3**

7. getting up late/trying out new sports/sub-aqua (**or** diving)/windsurfing (**any three**) **3**

3 School/college

1. she has two answers/liked her first school (or *collège*)/found her second school (or *lycée*) terrible (was not happy going there) **3**

2. it was near her house (500 m from her house)/she could go home at lunchtime/she knew everyone in her class well **3**

3. almost all nice/apart from German teacher (she was sarcastic)/her English teacher encouraged them to speak **3**

4. she had to get a train there **or** it was 20 km away/she had to leave home at 6.30/ate in canteen/got home at 7 p.m./still had homework/her friends were at another school/felt quite alone (**any five**)　　5

5. she wanted to/was in a bilingual class (special European class)/some of her lessons were in English/she thought it important to speak English (**any three**)　　3

6. the teachers were interesting/she learned a lot/got good marks (a good bac **or** school-leaving certificate)　　3

4　Tourism/home area

1. in Nice/south-east of France/a flat in the town centre　　3
2. great/always something to do/lots of friends there/weather almost always good　　4
3. his parents owned a restaurant/couldn't go away in summer　　2
4. couldn't get into clubs (discos)/needed ID at doors/tourists could get in without ID　　3
5. a small town (of 6,000 inhabitants)/south-east Scotland/is working　　3
6. friendly (everyone knows everyone)/gets invited out/near Edinburgh/rains too much/ you need a car (**any four**)　　4
7. tour the north of Scotland　　1

5　Leisure and healthy living

1. no/you don't see scenes in France like Saturday night here　　2
2. children used to get wine and water/more health-conscious (healthy) now/drink water or juice　　3
3. family parties/special occasions/when they are older (at least 12 or 13)　　3
4. they have more freedom/used to have to stay home in evening (after 6 or 6.30)/can go out now/that is when they buy beer　　4
5. it is quite dear/not very private (young people can't be by themselves)　　2
6. not quite (to a certain extent)/girls don't have as much freedom (have to go home earlier)/do more homework　　3
7. seeing young people totally drunk/younger than in France (12- or 13-year-olds)/drink stronger drinks/see them lying in the streets (**any three**)　　3

6　Family, friends, society

1. lives with mum and sister/grandparents live next door/aunt, uncle and cousins live 20 m away/father lives in next village　　4
2. his parents fought all the time/nobody was happy/his father got a new house (**any two**)　　2
3. he would prefer his father in the house/accepts it　　2
4. every day after school/at weekends　　2
5. father a teacher and helps with homework/mum works late/convenient for everyone　　3
6. likes his mum's parents/but they are strict/dad's parents live far away/sees them not very often or in holidays/they are great fun **or** not strict (**any three**)　　4
7. she is young (12)/good fun/they never fight/visits their cousins often (**any three**)　　3

7 Leisure and healthy living

1. grew up where the Tour de France passed/always loved it/in his blood (**any two**)   2
2. doesn't have time, likes music (going to concerts) as well   1
3. goes in a group/cycles 120 km/goes into hills (mountains)/it's exhausting (**any three**)   3
4. goes to a pub with the others/drink, talk, have a laugh (**any two**)/stays for an hour or so   3
5. football/plays on Wednesdays **or** plays for an hour **or** plays with four others (**any two**)   3
6. he likes it/have to run a lot/still is fun   3
7. folk **or** world music/Celtic music (**or** music of Scotland **and** Ireland)   2
8. the bagpipes   1
9. it's hard to play/finding somewhere to practise (where no one can hear him)   2

8 Careers

1. works in a bar/Thursdays 8–12/Saturdays for 8 hours   3
2. her flat is dear/needs extra money/likes to get out and meet people   3
3. she likes it/well-paid/nice atmosphere through no smoking/meets lots of people/goes out (to club) with them after work (**any three reasons**)   4
4. Friday mornings/getting up for work/annoying when there are drunks in bar   3
5. she stayed with her parents/no rent or food to buy/lived near uni **or** few transport costs   3
6. July and August/worked in a holiday camp (was an activity assistant)   2
7. everything was paid for (no expenses other than phone)/liked seeing the little ones enjoy themselves   2

9 Leisure and healthy living

1. the weather/it rains more **and** is colder (even in summer)   2
2. in France coffee, hot chocolate and bread/maybe cereal/in Scotland a hamburger or sausages, bacon and egg (**any two**)/or even nothing but a Coke   4
3. he hates fatty foods/would be worse in morning   2
4. most people keep on working/stay at work with sandwich and drink/might look at Internet/some go out jogging/eat very quickly afterwards (**any four**)   4
5. sees them in street/sandwich or chips in hand/not even sitting (**any two**)   2
6. had an hour and a half/went home at lunchtime/mum made lunch for him (**any two**)   2
7. relaxes for an hour/eats two courses (and coffee)   2
8. in France most restaurants offer French food/in Scotland hard to find Scottish food **or** Scottish national dish seems to be curry   2

LISTENING TRANSCRIPTS

Text One: Yvonne is being interviewed about her plans for the future.

Q   Yvonne, vous travaillez à présent à Glasgow: que faites-vous exactement?

Y   D'abord, je suis venue ici pour un an comme assistante dans une école à Glasgow, et ensuite j'ai trouvé du travail comme serveuse dans un bar, afin de pouvoir rencontrer d'autres jeunes.

Q   Vous êtes d'où en France?

Y   Je suis étudiante en fac à Lille, mais je suis originaire d'un petit village dans le Nord, Marchiennes, tout près de Lille, à trente kilomètres pour préciser, ou une demi-heure en train.

Q   Vous comptez retourner en France bientôt?

Y   Oui, bien sûr: je veux reprendre mes études en septembre, et ensuite je resterai encore deux ans pour finir, mais après j'ai l'intention de revenir en Écosse pour devenir professeur.

Q   Alors vous aimez les enfants en Écosse, évidemment ceux dans votre école?

Y   Ah oui, oui, la plupart oui: il y en a qui me posent des problèmes de temps en temps, en fait ils refusent de parler en classe et bien sûr il y a aussi ceux qui me demandent tout le temps 'Pourquoi est-ce que je dois apprendre le Français?', mais j'ai beaucoup d'élèves qui s'intéressent à la France, et voudraient y aller.

Q   Est-ce que vous comptez rester longtemps en Écosse, dès votre retour ici?

Y   Là, je ne sais pas: ça dépend de comment ça se déroule avec mon petit ami. J'ai rencontré quelqu'un ici, et si ça continue, eh bien je veux bien rester plus longtemps.

Q   Vous pourriez imaginer d'avoir une famille ici?

Y   Oui, bien sûr. Vous savez, Glasgow n'est pas tellement différente de Lille, et puis il y a des vols de l'Écosse à Lille ou en Belgique qui ne sont pas chers du tout, donc comme ça je pourrai rester en contact avec ma famille.

Q   Qu'est-ce qu'en pensent vos parents?

Y   Alors, pour ma mère, naturellement elle préférerait que je resterais en France, plus proche d'elle, mais elle accepte mes désirs, et mon père adore le golf, donc, il est content, car comme ça il peut venir n'importe quand faire un petit parcours de golf!

Text Two: Jacques talks about his experiences of holidays with his family and his friends.

Q   Jacques, quand êtes vous parti en vacances sans vos parents pour la première fois?

J   Alors, ça dépend: je suis parti pratiquement chaque année dès l'âge de treize ans en colonie de vacances avec mes copains, normalement dans le Midi. Là, c'était une visite organisée, il y avait des moniteurs, et nous on n'était pas vraiment indépendant. La première fois que je suis parti tout seul avec mes copains, j'avais dix-sept ans.

Q   Où êtes-vous allés?

J   On est allés en Bretagne à vélo pour faire du camping, et on a passé une semaine près de Saint Malo. Nous étions quatre, tous en première au lycée. On a fait cinquante kilomètres par jour, mais on restait toujours près de la mer, pour pouvoir nager chaque matin.

Q   Cela vous a-t-il plu?

J   C'était super: on s'est levé tard le matin, il n'y avait pas de pression pour visiter les monuments, et nous mangions ce que nous voulions quand nous voulions.

Q   Vous aimiez aller en vacances avec vos parents?

J   Ah oui, je m'entends bien avec ma famille, et on allait toujours dans une petite maison dans le Midi, au bord de la mer. J'avais beaucoup de liberté, parce qu'on connaissait tout le monde dans le village, et j'avais des amis là-bas.

Q   Il n'y avait jamais de problèmes?

J   Si, il y avait des règles pour les repas: je devais me lever à huit heures pour le petit déjeuner, et je devais toujours rentrer à une heure pour déjeuner, même si je voulais rester à la plage avec mes copains.

Q   Comment sont vos vacances aujourd'hui?

J   C'est très varié: quelquefois je pars en train avec mes parents une semaine dans cette maison, dans le midi, mais je pars aussi avec ma petite amie un peu plus loin. On part en avion, pour aller en Grèce ou en Espagne.

Q   Étes-vous actif en vacances?

J   Oui, bien que j'aime encore me lever tard. Je suis assez sportif, et j'aime pratiquer de nouveaux sports. L'année dernière j'ai appris la plongée sous-marine, et cette année je veux bien pratiquer de la planche à voile.

Text Three: Marie-Claire talks about her schooldays.

Q   Marie-Claire, est-ce que vous aimiez aller à l'école?

M   Alors là, j'ai deux réponses: mon collège, je l'aimais bien, mais lorsque je suis allée au lycée à l'âge de quinze ans, j'ai trouvé ça affreux, et je n'étais pas du tout contente de devoir y aller.

Q   Pourquoi aimiez-vous votre collège?

M   Eh bien, c'était tout près de la maison: nous habitions à cinq cent mètres du collège, donc je pouvais rentrer à midi pour déjeuner chez moi, et je connaissais très bien tout le monde dans ma classe.

Q   Vous aimiez aussi les professeurs?

M   Oui, ils étaient presque tous gentils, à part ma prof d'Allemand: elle était très sarcastique, et aimait trouver les fautes quand on parlait en classe. Mais mon prof d'Anglais était complètement différent: il nous encourageait tous à parler en Anglais tout le temps en classe.

Q   Et pourquoi le lycée était-il une expérience moins positive?

M   Ben, d'abord je devais prendre le train pour y aller, car c'était à vingt kilomètres de chez moi, ce qui voulait dire que je devais quitter la maison à six heures et demie, manger à la cantine, puis je ne rentrais le soir qu'à dix-neuf heures, et il me restait des devoirs à faire.

Q   Mais à part ça?

M   Presque tous mes copains sont allés dans un autre lycée, donc je me sentais assez isolée, car je voyageais seule le matin, et je ne rencontrais pas les autres lycéens après les cours.

Q   Mais vous êtes quand même restée là-bas?

M   Eh bien, je voulais le faire, parce que j'étais dans une classe européenne ou bilingue, on faisait quelques matières en anglais comme par exemple l'histoire, et ça j'appréciais beaucoup, parce que je trouvais ça important de bien parler anglais.

Q   C'était un bon lycée?

M   Ah oui, bien sûr, et les profs étaient intéressants, et puis j'ai beaucoup appris, et le plus important c'est que j'ai obtenu un bon bac, j'avais de bonnes notes: le problème était plutôt la distance et tout ce que cela voulait dire pour moi.

Text Four: Eric is talking about growing up in a big town.

Q   Éric, d'où est-ce que vous venez?

É   Je suis né à Nice, dans le sud-est de la France, et j'ai passé tout ma vie là avant d'aller à l'université. Cela veut dire que j'ai passé dix-neuf ans, dans un appartement dans le centre-ville.

Q   Et comment est-ce que vous avez trouvé ça?

É   J'ai trouvé ça formidable, car il y avait toujours quelque chose à faire, j'avais beaucoup d'amis qui habitaient pas trop loin, et puis il faisait beau presque tout le temps.

Q   Il n'y avait pas un côté négatif?

É   Pas vraiment: la seule chose peut-être c'était que mes parents tenaient un restaurant, donc on ne pouvait pas partir en vacances l'été comme les autres, mais j'avais des copains dans la même situation, et alors on savait s'amuser, il y avait la plage, la piscine, le terrain de foot, tout ça.

Q   Et c'est tout?

É   Eh bien, lorsque j'avais seize, dix-sept ans, ça me gênait qu'on n'aie pas le droit d'aller dans les boîtes, les discothèques, et parce que c'était une grande ville, l'entrer du boîtes était bien contrôlé, il fallait avoir sa carte d'identité. Mais on voyait les touristes, les jeunes Anglais par exemple, y entrer sans carte. C'était pas juste.

Q   Et où habitez vous maintenant?

É   Alors en ce moment, je suis dans une petite ville de six mille habitants dans le sud-est de l'Écosse. Je travaille là-bas.

Q   C'est un peu différent de Nice?

É   Ah oui, mais je l'aime bien cet endroit, même s'il pleut un peu trop pour moi. C'est très amical, tout le monde se connaît, et je suis invité le soir. Puis Édimbourg est à une heure en voiture. J'ai dû acheter une voiture, car il faut avoir une voiture ici, sinon on serait très isolé.

Q   Et vous comptez rester ici longtemps?

É   Non, non: je suis là pour dix mois, je trouve ça bien de se lever le matin et voir de la neige dans la rue, comme c'est arrivé quelquefois, mais je suis originaire d'une grande ville, et je retournerai à Nice au mois de septembre. Mais avant ça, je vais partir dans le nord de l'Écosse pendant deux mois pour visiter tout ce qu'il y a à visiter!

Text Five: Francine talks about young people and their attitude to drinking alcohol in France.

Q Francine, j'ai entendu que les jeunes en France ont commencé à boire de l'alcool comme les Britanniques: est-ce que vous avez remarqué cela vous-même?

F Il ne faut pas exagérer! Rien en France ne ressemble aux rues d'une grande ville en Angleterre ou en Écosse le samedi soir. Mais bien sûr, les jeunes ont tendance à boire entre eux maintenant plus qu'avant.

Q Est-ce qu'on a encore l'habitude comme dans les autres générations d'apprendre à boire en famille?

F Moins je crois, autrefois les petits enfants prenaient un verre de vin dilué avec de l'eau à table le soir, mais maintenant on est plus conscient de la santé des enfants, et on leur offre du jus de fruit ou de l'eau à table.

Q Alors les jeunes Français ne boivent plus de vin à table?

F Mais si, mais surtout à des fêtes de famille, ou pour les occasions exceptionnelles, comme les anniversaires, les mariages, des choses comme ça. Et même là, on commence plus tard, les enfants sont plus agés, ils ont au moins douze, treize ans maintenant.

Q Vous avez dit que les jeunes boivent entre eux: qu'est-ce que ça veut dire?

F Autrefois les jeunes avaient moins de liberté, ils devaient rester à la maison le soir après six heures, six heures et demie. Maintenant ils peuvent sortir le soir: c'est là qu'ils s'achètent des bières pour boire ensemble.

Q Ils ne vont pas au café?

F Pas forcément: les cafés, ça coûte assez cher et puis ce n'est pas très privé, les jeunes ne peuvent pas être entre eux. Donc on va au supermarché, on achète quelques cannettes de bière, et on va au parc.

Q C'est vrai pour les filles comme pour les garçons?

F Dans une certaine mesure: les filles n'ont pas encore autant de liberté que les garçons, elles doivent rentrer plus tôt, puis elles font aussi mieux leurs devoirs que les garçons, mais tout de même, on voit aussi des filles parfois dans les parcs!

Q Mais ce n'est pas comme ici en Grande Bretagne?

F Ah non, ici on voit les jeunes totalement ivres, beaucoup plus jeunes qu'en France, des jeunes quelquefois de douze ou treize ans, et en plus ils ne boivent pas de la bière, ils boivent de la vodka, des boissons fortement alcoolisées. On les trouve quelquefois inconscients dans les rues.

Text Six: Sylvain talks about how he gets on with the other members of his family.

Q   Sylvain, vous avez une grande famille?

S   Alors, oui et non. J'habite chez ma mère et ma sœur dans un petit village, mes grandparents habitent à côté, mon oncle, ma tante et mes cousines à trente mètres, et mon père dans le village voisin.

Q   Ça vous convient?

S   Eh bien, je aurais préféré que mon père habite encore chez nous, mais ça ne marchait plus, mes parents se bagarraient tout le temps, et personne n'était heureux. Donc il y a quatre ans il a trouvé une nouvelle maison et voilà. Je l'accepte.

Q   Vous le voyez souvent?

S   Ah oui, normalement j'y vais après l'école et je fais mes devoirs là-bas. Je rentre pour dîner. Le weekend on sort souvent ensemble, on joue au bowling, ou on va au cinéma le soir.

Q   Vous seulement?

S   Ah non, ma sœur Marie vient aussi: mon père est professeur, donc il peut l'aider avec ses devoirs, et ma mère doit travailler plus tard, donc c'est très pratique pour tout le monde.

Q   Et comment vous entendez-vous avec vos grandparents?

S   Les grandparents qui habitent à côté de chez nous, ce sont les parents de ma mère, et on se voit beaucoup. Je les aime bien, mais ils sont assez sévères, donc je préfère aller chez mon père. Mes autres grandparents je les vois rarement, car ils habitent loin de chez nous, mais on leur rend visite à Noël et pendant les grandes vacances. C'est super chez eux, et ils ne sont pas du tout sévères, on s'amuse très bien là-bas.

Q   Vous vous entendez bien, vous et votre sœur?

S   Ah oui: elle est assez jeune, elle a onze ans, mais elle est très rigolote, et on ne se dispute jamais. Elle est aussi souvent chez nos cousins.

Q   Vous les voyez beaucoup?

S   Moi pas tellement: mes cousines ont dix et onze ans, alors elles jouent beaucoup avec ma sœur, mais je ne trouve pas qu'on ait grand chose en commun. Alors je préfère être avec mes copains.

Text Seven: Vincent is talking about what he does in his spare time.

Q   Vincent, vous allez travailler en vélo: est-ce que vous faîtes cela parce que ça vous plaît, ou pour raison de santé?

V   Eh bien, j'ai toujours été passioné par le vélo: je suis originaire d'un petit village dans les Pyrénées, où le Tour de France passe tous les ans, donc le vélo on peut dire que j'ai ça dans mon sang. On regardait les cyclistes qui passaient à toute allure, puis on sautait sur son vélo.

Q   Alors, vous sortez aussi le weekend à vélo?

V   Ah oui, mais peut-être moins qu'avant: ce n'est pas tous les weekends que je sors, je n'ai plus le temps, parce que j'aime aussi beaucoup la musique, donc ça dépend de ce qu'il y a comme concerts, ou comme la musique à écouter.

Q   Vous ne pouvez pas combiner les deux, les balades à vélo et la musique?

V   Mais non: vous savez, quand je sors en vélo, je fais des randonnées de 120 kilomètres dans les collines et les montagnes, puis on sort en groupe aussi, donc après la randonnée et un passage au bar, je suis vraiment crevé.

Q   Vous faites du vélo, et après vous allez au bar?

V   Juste pour boire un verre, discuter de la journée et rigoler un peu. On reste une heure, une heure et demie, puis tout le monde rentre chez soi.

Q   C'est tout ce que vous faites comme sport?

V   Je joue aussi au foot tous les mercredis avec un groupe de copains: nous sommes cinq, et nous organisons des jeux contre d'autres équipes. On joue pendant une heure. C'est super bien, car on doit courir beaucoup mais on s'amuse en même temps.

Q   Vous avez parlé de la musique. Qu'est-ce que vous aimez comme musique?

V   Alors là, c'est très simple: j'adore la musique folklorique de tous les pays, la musique du monde. Surtout j'aime la musique celte de l'Irlande et de l'Écosse.

Q   Et jouez-vous vous-même d'un instrument?

V   À ce moment je suis en train d'apprendre à jouer de la cornemuse, je trouve celà très difficile: j'ai un professeur qui a beaucoup de patience, chez qui je vais deux fois par semaine. Mais trouver un endroit pour m'exercer, pour jouer où personne ne peut m'entendre, ça c'est le plus difficile pour moi.

Text Eight: Yvonne talks about her part-time job.

Q   Yvonne, vous travaillez le soir ou le weekend?

Y   Eh bien, les deux. Je travaille dans un bar les jeudis de huit heures jusqu'à minuit, puis tous les samedis, huit heures au total.

Q   Pourquoi est-ce que vous faites ce travail?

Y   Alors, il y a deux raisons: premièrement, je suis assistante dans une école à Glasgow, et mon appartement est très cher, donc je trouve que j'ai besoin de gagner un peu d'argent en plus. Et puis, ce qui est plus important, je peux sortir et rencontrer d'autres gens dans une bonne ambiance.

Q   Vous aimez votre petit boulot?

Y   Bien sûr: c'est bien payé, et puis maintenant qu'on n'a pas le droit de fumer dans les bars en Écosse, je trouve l'atmosphère plus supportable pour toute une soirée. En plus je rencontre beaucoup de monde lorsque je suis dans le bar, et après le travail on sort pour aller en boite de nuit ensemble.

Q   Il n'y a pas de problèmes avec le travail?

Y   Eh oui, je dois admettre que le vendredi, quand je dois me lever tôt pour aller à l'école, je suis très fatiguée et il me faut beaucoup d'énergie pendant mes cours. Et quelquefois il y a des gens qui boivent trop dans le bar, et ça peut être gênant, mais c'est assez rare, quand même.

Q   Est-ce que vous avez travaillé chez vous en France, pendant que vous étiez en fac?

Y   Non, pas vraiment. J'habite encore chez mes parents, et pour cette raison je n'ai pas de loyer à payer, ni d'argent à dépenser pour la nourriture. L'université est à deux kilomètres, donc le transport ne coûte pas cher.

Q   Alors vous vivez de votre argent de poche?

Y   Ah non, je travaille toujours pendant les grandes vacances, et je garde l'argent que je gagne: ça me donne normalement tout l'argent qu'il me faut pour l'année universitaire.

Q   Qu'est-ce que vous faites comme travail?

Y   Je suis monitrice dans une colonie de vacances. Je fais cela pendant les mois de juillet et d'août. C'est génial, parce que tout est payé, ma chambre, les repas, et je ne dépense rien, à part pour mon téléphone portable.

Q   Qu'est-ce que vous devez faire pour votre travail?

Y   Alors, on travaille avec les enfants qui sont là pendant quatre semaines. Les enfants avec lesquels je travaille ont entre six et douze ans. On leur propose des activités sportives et culturelles, on reste avec eux quand ils mangent, on les écoute parler de leurs problèmes entre beaucoup d'autres choses: c'est fatigant, mais cela vaut la peine, quand on voit les petits tellement s'amuser.

Text Nine: Vincent talks about the differences between eating in France and in Scotland.

Q   Vincent, vous êtes depuis un an ici en Écosse. Quelles sont pour vous les différences les plus marquantes entre la vie ici et la vie chez vous?

V   Je viens d'une ville dans le Midi, donc évidemment la différence la plus importante est le temps. Ici il pleut souvent, et il fait beaucoup plus froid, même en été. Mais à part cela, je dirais que la plus grande différence est la façon de se nourrir.

Q   Vous pouvez expliquer un peu?

V   Ça commence avec le petit déjeuner. Chez nous, on prend un café ou un bol de chocolat avec du pain. On peut aussi trouver des céréales. Mais ici j'ai vu des gens commencer la journée avec un hamburger, ou un grand plat plein de saucisses, d'œufs et de jambon. Puis j'en vois d'autres qui ne prennent rien d'autre qu'un Coca.

Q   Vous l'avez essayé vous-même, le petit déjeuner anglais?

V   Ah non, je ne pourrais pas le faire. J'ai déjà horreur des aliments trop gras, et le matin ça serait pire.

Q   Il y a d'autre différences?

V   Je dirais qu'il n'y a que des différences: à midi, pour déjeuner ici, la plupart de ceux que je rencontre ne s'arrêtent pas de travailler. Ils restent au bureau avec un sandwich et une boisson, peut-être ils surfent un peu sur l'Internet, mais c'est tout. Il y en a d'autres qui sortent pour faire du jogging, et après ils mangent vite quelque chose en deux, trois minutes. Même les élèves des écoles dans les alentours, je les vois dans la rue à midi avec un sandwich ou des frites à la main, ils ne s'asseyent même pas.

Q   Et ce n'est pas votre habitude?

V   Bien sûr que non! Quand j'étais au lycée, on avait une heure et demie pour déjeuner, et j'en profitais pour rentrer chez moi et manger confortablement quelque chose qu ma mère avait préparé.

Q   Et qu'est-ce que vous faites ici en Écosse?

V   Alors, on a une heure pour le déjeuner et je prends cette heure, je n'en sacrifie rien au travail, je me détends. Je mange un plat cuisiné et un dessert, et après je prends un café. Je reste Français!

Q   Comment trouvez-vous les restaurants ici?

V   Là aussi je vois beaucoup de différences. Chez nous, la plupart des restaurants offrent un repas français. Il y a bien sûr des restaurants italiens et vietnamiens ou chinois, mais c'est à peu près tout. Ici, on a des difficultés à trouver un restaurant qui propose des plats écossais. Le plat principal écossais me semble être un curry.

Q   Qu'est-ce que vous en pensez?

V   Personellement, je suis content: je peux découvrir un tas de cuisines différentes: ici j'ai mangé pour la première fois dans un restaurant mexicain, et je mange régulièrement dans un restaurant végétarien, chose que je ne ferais jamais chez moi, même si ça existait.

SPEAKING

Introduction

Speaking is worth **25 per cent** of your overall Higher result. You will have to carry out only one Speaking assessment, normally about two months before your exams, and probably in the month of March: this assessment will consist of a presentation by you, with a follow-up discussion on this and related topics with your teacher. The topic for the presentation will be set by you and your teacher together, and the whole assessment will be marked by your teacher. It will be recorded, and may be sent off to SQA for assessment/moderation, or it may not. You will not know in advance whether it will in fact be sent off, so just assume that it will be. This Speaking assessment will also count as the Speaking assessment for the Language Unit.

The rules for the assessment are quite clear: there will be a presentation, lasting up to two minutes, which gives you a chance to start off the assessment well and confidently. To help you through, you will be allowed to use notes consisting of a certain number of words: **five headings of up to eight words each**. This presentation is worth 10 marks, or 10 per cent of your final award. You will start off the discussion in this topic area, but will move on to other topic areas you have covered during the Higher course. The discussion is worth 15 marks, or 15 per cent of your final award. Your presentation will be graded according to 'grade descriptions', that is, criteria which are in Appendix Six, set out so that you can see what is expected of you. Look carefully at these when preparing your presentation and discussion.

The second part of the assessment will be a discussion, which will cover several of the topic areas you have looked at during your Higher French studies. The discussion will normally last about five minutes. This discussion will be marked following the same grade descriptions as the presentation.

In this chapter we will look at the two types of task in detail, and give you advice and support on preparing for the tasks you are facing.

The presentation

For this assessment, as for the prepared talk at Standard Grade Credit or the presentation at Intermediate 2, you will have to talk on a subject of your choice for up to two minutes: you can prepare this well in advance, and learn it so that you can be absolutely sure of what you have to do. You should also think carefully about your learning style, and whether a selection of words to use as notes to guide you through your presentation is the way to go, or just learning by heart. Some people find it useful to have five cue cards, each with a number of words to jog the memory. Others find that the first eight words of each section work best. It is important you find your own style.

You must be reasonably accurate in your use of French, and use tenses and a variety of structures well. You are expected to expand beyond the kind of vocabulary and ideas you used at Standard Grade. The presentation should have a clear structure, with a beginning and an end. Your opinions are very important, and you should also include reasons for some of these opinions. You can see examples of this later on in this chapter.

Planning your talk

You and your teacher should discuss the topic area you want to use for your presentation. You should choose an area you are comfortable with, but one which allows you to display your knowledge of French, and gives opportunities to include some good vocabulary and structures.

When you have a subject for your presentation, try to break it down into three to five sections, and prepare each one separately: this will make it easier to remember, as well as giving you structure. You are allowed five headings of eight words each as support, so these key words should settle you into each section of your talk: this is handy, as, if you get nervous and a bit mixed up in one part, you can recover in the next part with the help of your key words.

Once you've structured your talk, focus on the actual language you will use. Here are a few dos and don'ts!

Dos

◆ Do look at the texts you have been working from for good ideas you can use. These texts will be at the level you should be working at.

◆ Do make sure you understand what you are saying, or it will be very difficult to remember it properly. Use complex language, yes, but only language you are comfortable with.

◆ Do think about your pronunciation: record yourself and listen to what you sound like. Could you sound more French?

◆ Do share your drafts with your teacher, to get any suggestions or corrections made, and do this well in advance!

◆ Do use a variety of structures: start collecting these in a notebook or in an area of your folder or computer.

◆ Do vary your tenses, and put in complex sentences, using a variety of different joining words or conjunctions such as *parce que*, *car* or *quand*. If you can, use some of the conjunctions followed by the subjunctive (advice on this is in the 'Grammatical structures' section of Chapter 14).

◆ Do give your opinion at every opportunity, and work at having different ways of saying what you think. Look at the 'Giving opinions and reasons' section of Chapter 14.

Don'ts X

- Don't leave the preparation to the last minute! If you start your preparation early, you'll be able to ask your teacher for advice on any vocabulary or grammar you're unsure of. That means not just the week before, but a month before.

- Don't always stick to safe, simple language. It may be easier, but won't get the best grades. Try out some of the more impressive sentences you've come across. Note down useful vocabulary and phrases you've seen elsewhere under appropriate topic headings so that you can reuse them in your speaking tests.

- Just as at Standard Grade, don't use lists of things, such as school subjects, places in town or favourite foods, to try to make your talk longer: this will count against you.

Presentation topics

The topic areas from which you will be working are the topic areas of the Higher course, which are listed in Appendix One. Although the presentation and initial part of the discussion will be on the topic of your choice, you need to be able to deal with any of these areas, as the conversation may well go into any of them, so you must be prepared. Discuss with your teacher how this will go, but remember you will not be expected to cover areas you have not yet dealt with in class as part of your Higher course.

How should you choose a topic? There are several things you should think about:

- Choose a topic area you are comfortable with, and know something about.

- Make sure your chosen area allows you to get in a variety of tenses and structures, and allows you to put in opinions and feelings and explain the reasons for these opinions.

- Make sure it is not too simple, only allowing you to use the kind of language which would be appropriate for Standard Grade: this is a particular danger with topics like family and school. Your daily routine or what you are studying at school are not likely to give you enough chance to express yourself.

- You might want to choose the topic area you have been dealing with most recently, as it will be fresh in your mind.

- You might want to base your presentation on a small area of a topic you have dealt with, allowing you to talk about this topic in a wider context in the conversation: in health, for instance, you could talk about the fact that so many girls smoke, and what can be done about it. This means you can go on to talk about diet, problems with drinking, and exercise.

Let us look at some possible presentations, one from each topic area. The next section will guide you through the process involved in preparing for and carrying out the assessment for three specific topics: you can follow the same pattern for a presentation of your own choice. You should also look at Chapter 12 (Personal Response Writing) for further help on different specific areas.

Example presentations

We will consider the following:

1. l'importance du sport dans la vie;
2. boulot et bac;
3. les voyages.

1 L'importance du sport dans la vie

This topic comes from the lifestyles theme, and covers aspects of leisure and healthy living, two subtopics from the theme. Using this as a presentation topic will allow you to use both the first and the third person, give opinions and justify these, and use good phrases from the source texts you are using. It should also allow you to give conflicting points of view.

Your first step should be a kind of brainstorming: look at your source texts and select a variety of really good phrases or ideas. Look at these in turn and try to identify a pattern or storyline to follow, to give your presentation some structure. Then to break your task into areas. You could start with a section in which you talk about the importance of health, then have a section in which you talk about how sport can help people maintain it (and include a reference to what you think yourself), move on to where there are problems with this, and finish off with what people (and you) should be doing to improve things. If you have a textbook, you could use this for source material, or you could look on the internet for supporting material.

The first section might sound something like this.

> *De nos jours, on parle beaucoup de l'importance de la santé pour les jeunes: on pense à ce qu'on offre aux jeunes dans les cantines scolaires, on essaie d'interdire aux gens de fumer dans les lieux publics, il y a beaucoup de publicité à la télévision et au cinéma pour persuader les gens de penser à leur santé.*

This allows you to introduce the topic, and can also serve as the lead-in to later questions in the conversation. It is also general, and so avoids using *je* for just now. The second section can then let you move from the general to the particular. Here is an example.

> *Il est important de penser à ce qu'on peut faire pour garder la santé, et une des choses les plus importantes est de rester en forme. À l'écoles on essaie d'offrir aux élèves un minimum de deux heures de sport par semaine, mais cela n'est qu'un début. Personnellement, je trouve qu'il vaut mieux pratiquer une activité sportive chaque jour, afin qu'on puisse se maintenir en forme et développer son corps.*

This has allowed you to give opinions, and justify them. It has also allowed you to use a conjunction, *afin que*, which is followed by the subjunctive for added value! If that is a step too far, you could have said *afin de se maintenir en forme*.

The next section allows you to give some structure, by moving to problems, the other side of the argument, and also to personalise the presentation.

Il m'est quand même quelquefois assez difficile de trouver le temps pour toute cette activité: souvent j'ai beaucoup de devoirs, ou je dois travailler, car j'ai un petit boulot. Des fois quand je veux faire du footing il pleut, et je n'ai plus envie de sortir.

You have left in some hints for where the later discussion can go: your part-time job, or your work at school. It is important to add in the little words and phrases which make your French flow better, words like *quand même*, *quelquefois*, *assez*.

For the final section, you need to come to a conclusion, as well as giving an answer to the problems in the third paragraph. This section is your chance to show off all your ways of expressing opinions and making demands.

Mais il faut tout de même persister, car la santé est tellement importante pour notre avenir: il serait trop facile de dese laisser aller, de rester assis devant la télé pour faire partie des statistiques de l'obésité en Écosse. Nous devons donc changer comme nous menons nos vies, si nous voulons devenir un pays sain, un pays qui réussit dans les compétitions sportivs. Aux sports, citoyens!

2 Boulot et bac

This topic comes from the education and work theme, and allows you talk about both school and your part-time jobs: it will link into your future, allowing you to prepare an area for the discussion which follows on. Think about how you are going to structure your presentation: perhaps you might start off by saying what you are studying and how much homework you have. Then you could move on to talking about your job,

saying why you work. The next section could be about the clashes that sometimes occur, and you might finish off with the hope that it will all work out right in the end!

Let us look at the first section, and remember not to go for lists in this area!

À présent je fais mes Highers, mon bac, afin de pouvoir aller plus tard à l'université, si j'y réussis. Je fais quatre Highers, et il me faut faire deux heures de devoirs chaque soir, et même le week-end aussi! La matière la plus difficile, qui m'offre tellement de devoirs, est les maths, mais probablement, c'est que je ne suis pas doué en maths. À mon avis, le plus facile, c'est bien sûr le Français, mais là j'aime la prof.

This has given you the chance to put in some opinions, express a hope, and give reasons. In the next section you can try to move away from just *je*.

La plupart des élèves dans ma classe ont comme moi un petit boulot. Nous travaillons pour gagner de l'argent, car comme ça on peut se payer des vêtements ou sortir le week-end. Le boulot nous offre de l'indépendance: nous ne dépendons plus de nos parents pour notre argent de poche. Moi, je travaille dans un supermarché le samedi et deux soirs par semaine, au total 14 heures chaque semaine.

This leads you into the clashes, and again try to generalise it, talking about others as well.

Mes copains de classe et du travail ont quelquefois d'assez gros problèmes à intégrer les devoirs et le boulot: souvent il arrive qu'on doit faire des heures supplémentaires le même jour que l'on doit rédiger un devoir pour le prof d'Anglais. Si on refuse les heures supplémentaires, on risque de perdre son emploi, mais évidemment, si on ne prépare pas ses devoirs, on risque la colère du prof, et de ne pas réussir à ses examens.

Remember to keep putting in the little extra words, like *assez* and *évidemment*, which make your language flow better. Now, in the last section, a chance to change tenses and introduce conditional and future, as well as a subjunctive if you feel comfortable with this.

Naturellement, je fais de mon mieux pour intégrer les deux, donc je ferai mes devoirs normalement à l'avance, pour éviter des conflits. Mon espoir est que je continuerai à réussir, et je voudrais bien continuer de gagner de l'argent, mais je n'aimerais pas que mes notes soient endommagées par mon boulot, donc je ferai bien attention dans l'avenir, parce que pour moi le plus important sera de pouvoir aller en fac l'année prochaine.

3 Les voyages

This topic comes from the theme 'the wider world', and allows you to bring in a variety of tenses and structures, mentioning past travels and your future plans. You might start with a general statement about how you love travelling, and why; then move on to mention a journey you particularly liked or disliked, and finish up with your plans for next summer, mentioning who you are travelling with. The first section could look like this:

J'habite une petite ville en Écosse, et je l'aime bien, mais quand même j'adore faire des voyages, surtout de longs voyages à l'étranger. J'aime voyager pour un tas de raisons, d'abord parce que j'aime les voyages mêmes, être dans un train ou un avion. J'aime aussi rencontrer des gens que je ne connais pas, me faire de nouveaux amis. Finalement, j'aime pouvoir parler une autre langue.

That section allowed you to put together a list of three reasons, but introduce them with different words: you could also have used *premièrement, deuxièmement, troisièmement*. These kind of words help you remember what comes next. For the next section, let us look at two different ways of proceeding, both allowing you to introduce past tenses.

Mais je me souviens d'un voyage qui était moins réussi. Je suis parti avec l'école pour passer une semaine dans les Alpes, et nous avons eu un tas de problèmes. Pour commencer, le bus était peu confortable, et tout le monde se sentait malade pendant le voyage, qui a en plus duré vingt-trois heures. Puis l'hôtel était très sale, et les repas étaient vraiment dégoûtants. Enfin les professeurs se sont fâchés, car quelques élèves ont bu de l'alcool. Mais j'ai appris une chose importante: je ne repartirai jamais avec l'école.

Again, you have produced a list of reasons with different introductory words, which will help you learn the presentation: you have also shown that you can use the two different past tenses correctly, and finished off with a future tense. You have also given reasons, and used complex sentences with conjunctions, which gives the necessary structures for a good grade.

Now let us look at the final part. Most of the first two paragraphs were with *je*, although they also used the third person. You should change this and perhaps use *nous*.

> *Cette année, je veux partir avec mes parents en France: nous voulons aller dans le Midi, pour préciser à la Côte d'Azur. Nous irons à un camping, parce que comme ça c'est moins cher. Je sais qu'il y a des désavantages de voyager avec ses parents, mais nous nous entendons bien, et ce sera probablement la dernière fois que nous partirons ensemble, car l'année prochaine, mes copains et moi, on compte aller ensemble en Espagne après notre bac. Là, nous nous amuserons bien!*

This final paragraph also allows you to lead the conversation which follows into areas such as advantages and disadvantages of travelling with parents and friends, how you get on with your family, and your friends: this way you can have a certain amount of control over what happens next!

The follow-up discussion

Remember that the presentation is under your total control, and it should allow you to get started successfully and settle your nerves. Next comes the discussion, which will start in the topic area you have used in the presentation, but will go beyond that. This is less predictable, but you can still retain a certain amount of control over what happens and where the conversation goes. If you can give full answers to the questions, and also ask some questions of your own, then you should expect to answer something like twelve to fifteen questions in the time allocated: shorter answers will inevitably lead to more questions, and are less likely to let you show off all the things which could get you good grades.

You can start off the conversation by leaving some good starting points in your presentation for where the conversation goes next. This makes it easy for the 'interlocutor', normally your teacher, to ask the first questions, and for you to have a chance to prepare your answers. So in the topic '*L'importance du sport dans la vie*', you left hanging the topics of your part-time job and your work at school. In '*Boulot et bac*', you also left open the subject of school, but in addition your future. In '*Les voyages*', it was advantages and disadvantages of travelling with parents and friends, how you get on with your family, and your friends generally.

When preparing for the conversation, it is important that you allow yourself the opportunity to demonstrate exactly the same things as you did in the presentation, namely the control of structures and vocabulary, a variety of tenses, a structure to the answer, opinions and reasons, and so on. The best way to do this is to make your answers longer, which has the added advantage that you will have to answer fewer questions! If you have thought of some longer answers, it also means that other answers can be quite short: this is useful when you cannot think of an answer, or when you are going down a road the teacher is taking you, but you do not want to go!

One useful thing to think of is the one–two–three approach: this means every answer should have three parts. If you are asked, for instance, *Qu'est-ce que tu fais dans ton boulot?*, then your answer could go:

1. *Je travaille dans un supermarché qui s'appelle …*
2. *Là, je travaille normalement à la caisse.*
3. *C'est un travail assez bien payé.*

This allows the next question to be one which asks you what you think of your job. Again, when giving your opinion, stick to the one–two–three approach.

1. *Je trouve le travail dans le supermarché assez ennuyeux*

2. *parce que travailler à la caisse est très répétitif*

3. *mais mes copains travaillent là aussi, donc ça va tout de même.*

This has given you the opportunity to give reasons and use conjunctions. You might also have prepared an answer to the question *Depuis combien de temps est-ce que tu travailles là?* The one–two–three approach should make it easier to give longer answers, but it also makes it easier to remember your answers, as you can count them off either mentally or on your fingers as a memory aid. So, after having given one answer, you might think it a good opportunity to add another answer here, and this is another way to help you control the conversation. Therefore, you could add this answer to the previous one, and it can still sound natural!

1. *Je travaille dans le supermarché depuis un an.*

2. *J'ai commencé au mois de mai, après mes examens,*

3. *parce que je voulais gagner de l'argent.*

This answer also invites the question 'What do you do with the money?', to which you would have prepared the answer in advance.

In the '*Boulot et bac*' topic, one of the obvious questions was *Qu'est-ce que tu veux faire après ton bac?* You have a choice here, as you could talk about your immediate plans, such as going on holiday with your friends, which allows you to develop this topic area, or you could talk about your plans to work, go to university or take a year out. If you stick to the latter, when you have said everything you can think of about university and so on, you can then add to your answer a sentence something like *Mais dans le futur immédiat, je veux partir en vacances avec mes copines cet été.* This will lead the conversation into this area, which you can have prepared.

Let us look at another one–two–three answer to the question about your future plans.

1. *Je ne suis pas certain de ce que je ferai.*

2. *Ou je pourrais aller directement à l'université, si je réussis à mes examens,*

3. *ou je pourrai trouver un travail pour un an, les deux possibilités ont des avantages et des désavantages.*

Again, this leads the conversation where you want: you can have prepared answers about the advantages and disadvantages, which allows you to get in good structures, reasons and opinions. And remember, when you think you have exhausted this topic, you can lead on to the next area: the immediate future. Look back at the suggested presentation for the topic area '*Les voyages*' for further ideas.

In the topic area '*Les voyages*', one of the possible lead-on questions was *Comment est-ce que tu t'entends avec tes parents?* Even if you are not asked this question, you will always be able to squeeze in the answer, by saying at some point *Mais quand même, j'aime les voyages avec mes parents, car on s'entend bien*, and then going on to give your prepared answer. Here is a possible one–two–three answer to the question:

1. *Généralement, on s'entend très bien, je crois,*

2. *bien que ça soit de temps en temps un peu difficile (or: bien sûr, c'est de temps en temps un peu difficile),*

3. *surtout quand je rentre trop tard le soir: mes parents s'inquiètent.*

This has allowed you to put in a subjunctive, if you want, and put together a structured answer. Another possible question was about your friends; it may go something like this: *Est-ce qu tu as beaucoup d'amis?* The one–two–three answer could be:

1. *Oui, nous sommes un grand groupe de copains, tous à l'école,*

2. *et nous faisons beaucoup de choses ensemble*

3. *mais évidemment j'ai deux copines qui me sont les plus proches.*

This answer lets you invite the next question, about the two special friends. You can either wait for that question or just insert the answer here, to give you a much longer answer.

What is really important about the conversation is that it flows, and is a real conversation: you have to really answer the questions that are put to you, and to ask some of your own. For this to happen, you must be very confident that you understand the question put to you, and know how to ask questions. If you do not understand the question, don't try to bluff or guess, and do not under any circumstances blurt out an answer you have learned and hope for the best! Much better is to ask for help in French, and if you ask properly you need not bring your grade down at all: in fact, you might be able to improve it. Here are some ways of asking for help, starting off easy and getting more complicated, but better!

♦ *Pardon?*

♦ *Voulez-vous répéter, s'il vous plaît?*

♦ *Je n'ai pas très bien compris.*

♦ *Là, je n'ai pas compris: pourriez-vous répéter la question?*

♦ *Excusez-moi, pourriez-vous reposer la question? Je ne suis pas certain(e) de ce que vous voulez savoir.*

DIRECTED WRITING

Introduction

There are two pieces of writing in the Higher French external exam. You will have to write a description of a trip you made to a French-speaking country (Directed Writing), and you will have to give your opinion on topics connected with the Listening assessment (Personal Opinion Writing). The Directed Writing is what we are going to look at here. The Directed Writing paper is given to you at the same time as the Reading paper, and you have one hour and forty minutes in which to do both. That means you should allow about forty minutes to plan, write and proofread your piece. This is quite possible, as much of what you will have to write is very predictable, and you can plan for this in advance.

The task will be based on a scenario given in English. You will be required to provide specified information in a piece of writing of 150–180 words: the scenario is always given with a number of bullet points which you have to cover. You will be able to use a dictionary while doing the exam. The scenario always involves you describing a trip to a French-speaking country which took place some time in the past. This is to make sure you write in the past and demonstrate your skill in using all of the past tenses! Remember that when using the perfect tense, as well as adjectives, sometimes it will matter whether you are male or female, so make sure your endings are consistent.

You can use textbooks and work you have already produced to guide you in your preparation, and you can work from guidelines provided by your teacher. This means you can really plan out a lot of what you want to write before the day of the exam.

Your writing will be graded according to how well it demonstrates a sense of structure, control of grammar and how it addresses the bullet points. The way your work will be judged is given in the Grade Descriptions for Writing: these are set out in Appendix Four so that you can see what is expected of you. You will get a grade based on the quality of your writing, and then you will have 2 marks subtracted from the total for each bullet point you miss out: that means it is important not to miss out any bullet points, but to address each one in your writing. Tick them off on your exam paper as you go, to make sure you have covered every one, and indeed each part of them.

Sample Directed Writing paper

Let us look at an example of a Directed Writing paper: after this, we will look at the kind of general basic answers that you should be prepared to write, which should help you write an essay based on this question. When you have done that, take it to your teacher and ask him/her (very nicely, of course) to mark it.

Your school/college has established links and an exchange programme with a school/college in a small town in France. You were sent as part of a group to visit the French school/college.

On your return, you have been asked to write **in French** an account of your experiences for inclusion in the foreign-language section of your school/college magazine.

You must include the following information and **you should try to add** other relevant details:

- how you travelled and where you stayed;
- where the French school/college was situated and what the area was like;
- what happened when you first arrived;
- what your impressions were of the school/college;
- what excursions were organised for your group; and
- how you intend to continue the links with the French school/college.

Your account should be 150–180 words in length.

You will see that there are six bullet points you have to cover, as well as bearing in mind the instructions at the top. This means you cannot simply prepare a piece of writing, learn it, and then write it out again in the exam. Some of the bullet points are very predictable, but others will be unique to that exam, so you must be prepared to be flexible. You have to write 150–180 words in total, so a good rule of thumb is that each bullet point should have at least 25 words, with one or two being a bit longer. If your writing is unbalanced, you might lose points. This guideline also makes it easier to keep track of how much you are writing, rather than always recounting words and wasting time!

What will you find easiest to prepare? Here is a list of things that are liable to come up:

- how you got there (you can prepare this in advance, but be ready to change method of transport and times or dates);
- who you travelled with (again, be ready to change the details for this);
- what the journey was like;
- where you stayed (this could be the house, the hostel, the town, or the area);
- what you did during the day when you were there (this is an area where you will have to have different ideas ready, as you may be on a work-experience, school exchange, sports trip, school visit, or family visit);
- what you did in the evenings (more predictable!);
- what you thought of the place or the people with whom you stayed;
- whether you will do such a visit again, and why (this makes you include a future or conditional tense); and
- how you will keep in touch with people you met.

Let us look at these one at a time. First, how you got there.

If we assume you went to France, you can choose your method of transport, unless the question actually specifies the method. You should also be able to put in when you went, as this is relevant. However, you might also have to change these details! This is likely to be the beginning of your writing, so start off well to impress the examiner.

> *L'année dernière, au mois de juin, je suis parti pour aller à Lille, dans le nord-est de la France. Nous y sommes allés en train, et bien sûr, on a pris l'Eurostar de Londres à Lille.*

This is quite straightforward, and is already over 30 words. We have also varied the subject and the structures, so that every sentence does not start off with *je*. To this you could add opinions (*Le voyage était très long, mais on s'est bien amusés*). This allows you to give opinions, put in a different tense, and use a reflexive verb with the correct ending. That is enough, so now on to the second bullet point, who you went with:

> *Le voyage de deux semaines était organisée par notre prof de Français, Mme Vernier, et toute ma classe de Higher a participé au voyage: nous étions donc seize élèves et deux professeurs. Dans le groupe se trouvaient mes deux meilleurs copines, Sara et Beckie.*

Again, you have more than enough words, and you have used two different past tenses.

Now to how the journey was, and the chance to put in opinions and reasons for the opinions, if you have not already done this:

> *Le voyage était assez long (douze heures en tout), surtout parce qu'on devait changer de gare à Londres, mais quand même on s'est bien amusé, car tout le monde avait son lecteur MP3, Sophie avait apporté son lecteur DVD et nous avons acheté tous les magazines disponibles à la gare!*

That section is longer, and would only go in if you were asked to describe the journey, as it could otherwise be seen as using irrelevant material. You must make sure your answers are relevant to the questions asked.

Another likely area is to talk about where you stayed: this might be a family home, a hostel or other such accommodation. If staying with a family, this can be very straightforward – just a simple description of the house and your room, with, of course, an opinion!

> *Ma famille habitait une petite maison à deux kilomètres de l'école, avec trois chambres. Moi, j'avais une petite chambre pour moi, et j'en étais contente, car chez moi je dois partager une chambre avec ma sœur.*

If you are in student accommodation, the answer can be very similar:

> *J'étais logé dans un bâtiment à deux kilomètres de l'université. Moi, j'avais une petite chambre pour moi, et j'en étais content, car chez moi je dois partager une chambre avec mon frère.*

One of the main parts of your directed writing will be to describe what you did when you were there: this will depend very much on the scenario set at the top of the task, but there will be common structures you can use whatever the scenario. There are two different areas here as well: the first is what you did during the day, the second is what you did in your leisure time.

First, let us look at what you could write about the daytime: this will depend very much on whether you are describing a visit to a school, family and so on, or whether you are working. If you are visiting someone, then you will be able to use the following kind of language:

Tous les jours on a fait des visites: on est allés par exemple au centre-ville de Lille pour voir les musées, et on a fait une visite en bus à une brasserie, où on a pu essayer de la bière française: c'était amusant de voir nos profs avec un verre à la main, et j'ai pris une photo pour faire chanter [blackmail] *Mme Vernier!*

If you are visiting a family, use this as an opportunity to use third-person verbs, as well as *nous* and *on*, as this gets away from always using *je*. Note that this answer is for a boy: for a girl, probably *ma corres* and *emmenée*.

Les parents de mon corres m'ont emmené en Belgique, où on a pris un bateau-mouche à Bruges: c'était extra, car on a vu tous les canaux.

If you are attending a school, then you can describe the school, the teachers and what you thought of some of the lessons:

Le lycée était très grand: il y avait 1800 élèves en tout dans un bâtiment immense, et tellement de professeurs que je ne reconnaissais personne. J'ai participé à des cours d'Anglais (marrant) et de maths (épatant). On n'a pas pu faire de sport, ce qui était dommage.

If you are working, or taking part in a work-experience, then you can describe your job and what you thought of it. Note that the following answer is for a girl:

J'ai travaillé dans un hôtel comme serveuse, ce qui était assez difficile, car tout le monde parlait Français, bien sûr. Le travail était dûr, mais j'ai reçu beaucoup de pourboires, donc j'étais finalement très contente.

You are also likely to be asked to write about what you did during your free time, in the evenings or at the weekends: this might be mixed up with what you did generally, but you can probably use this section whatever the topic. One suggestion follows, but you should prepare your own and have it ready to use!

Je suis allé au cinéma une fois avec un groupe de copains: pour moi, c'était la première fois que je voyais un film en Français sans sous-titres, et je n'en ai pas compris grand chose.

You are very likely to be asked about your impressions of the other people there, or how you got on with them, or else what you thought of where you stayed. This is pretty predictable, with just a few changes necessary to meet the context. For instance, for your fellow students:

Je me suis très bien entendu avec les autres étudiants. Ils étaient tous sympa, et nous restons en contact par mail et par sms. Surtout j'ai aimé Vincent, qui a passé beaucoup de temps avec moi, et qui m'a aidé à parler Français.

Or your host family:

Je me suis très bien entendu avec ma famille. Ils étaient tous sympa, et nous restons en contact par mail et par lettre. Surtout j'ai aimé la mère de mon corres, qui a passé beaucoup de temps avec moi, et qui m'a aidé à parler Français.

You will usually be asked as a final bullet point to use future and/or conditional tenses, by saying how you will keep in touch, whether you would do the visit again, or how you will be helped in the future by your experience. This could be done by giving your plans for next year, when you will complete the exchange or go back to the same place, by describing how you will keep in touch, or by saying how much better your French is and what a confident mature person you have become! First of all, plans for the future:

En septembre mon corres reviendra chez nous avec sa classe: ils vont passer dix jours chez notre école, ce qui sera fantastique! Pour l'instant, on va s'écrire des mails chaque semaine, et bien sûr j'enverrai des SMS [messages texte] si j'ai de l'argent dans mon phone portable! L'année prochaine, je voudrais bien retourner là-bas tout seul pour passer l'été à travailler et apprendre plus de Français.

And now, boasting about how wonderful your French has become! Into this you have even managed to get a subjunctive: *bien que j'aie.*

J'ai parlé beaucoup, et bien que j'aie fait pas mal d'erreurs, j'ai aussi fait de sérieux progrès. Cela m'aidera l'année prochaine, quand je compte aller à l'université pour faire des études de Français.

Now let us look at the bullet points from the example. You were asked to include:

◆ how you travelled and where you stayed

This was covered in the work above.

◆ where the French school/college was situated and what the area was like

You will have to make up something about the area, although the other part has been covered.

◆ what happened when you first arrived.

This area is not covered by what we have looked at: you will have to be ready in the exam to do some things for the first time! Follow the pattern, by saying something along the lines of 'When we arrived in Lille, I met the family of my penpal. I was afraid, but they were very nice'. Be simple and straightforward in the bits that you have not thought through before: do not be tempted to use the dictionary too much – stick to language you know is correct. You can include good bits elsewhere to get the best mark possible, as long as you do not let the writing down by making a mess of this section.

◆ what your impressions were of the school/college

Help for this you should find above.

◆ what excursions were organised for your group

Again, this is something you should have ready, as it is always liable to be there: you could take the text above, or have your own versions ready.

◆ how you intend to continue the links with the French school/college

This was also covered above. It is something you should have ready and be able to put in quickly.

So we hope that you can see that the Directed Writing is not just a leap in the dark: you can have most of the bullet points well prepared, as long as you are able to be flexible. Now try to write an answer for the sample paper, and show your work to your teacher.

What you should do next is look at the Directed Writing in other past papers, which you can either buy or ask your teacher to show you. Look at the bullet points in each of them, and see how much of each of these papers you can prepare in advance. You should also look at the bullet points that present unexpected material, and plan how you would answer them.

PERSONAL RESPONSE WRITING

Introduction

Remember that you will have to produce two pieces of writing during your Higher exam, and that writing altogether makes up **25 per cent** of your overall mark. The Personal Response Writing is the shorter piece and is worth 10 marks. This piece of writing is a personal response to the topic that is the focus of the Listening paper. This means you will not know in advance what the subject of the Personal Response is, and you will have about forty minutes in the exam to plan and produce the final piece of writing.

However, this is not as bad as it sounds. First, you will only have to write 120–150 words. Second, you will have covered the themes and topics of the course over the year of your Higher studies, so that the topic will not be one that is new to you. And, finally, as this is a personal response, which means you have to give your opinion, you can have a lot of your answer prepared in advance: you should develop a range of good phrases which you can adapt to any topic.

Let us look at the topics, set out in the following grid, which have come up over the last few years.

Year	Topic
2006	School: what makes a good school; are you going to college or beginning work after school?
2005	Sport: what can you do where you live; is sport important for you; should young people do more sport?
2004	Future: your future plans; why learn a foreign language?
2003	Freedom: do you have enough freedom on holiday, at school and at home?
2002	Where you would like to live: will you stay or move away?
2001	Health and fitness: what do you do; are they important?
2000	Advantages of learning a foreign language
1999	Living in town as opposed to the country
1998	Living with your parents: advantages and disadvantages

You can see that there are some common themes which run through the past papers, and that school, where you live, your attitude to health, and holidays are really common. These are the topics that you would expect to cover in depth over the course of your Higher year, and you should make a point of collecting relevant phrases and sentences on these topics to give you a bank of material to work from when preparing these tasks. You are also very likely to be asked about the future, so make sure you have some future and conditional verbs and phrases prepared. You will find a full list of the potential topics in Appendix One.

Your writing will be marked according to how well it demonstrates a sense of structure, control of grammar, variety of vocabulary, and also how relevant it is! The way your performance will be judged is given in the Criteria for Personal Response Writing. These are set out in Appendix Five so that you can see what is expected of you. However, what lets many people down is that they do not answer properly the actual questions which are given in the Listening paper: we will look at this later.

Planning your writing

Once you've been given your topic area, focus on the actual language you will use. Look carefully at the leading questions, to make sure you answer them in your response. These are not all you need to think about, but your personal response must address these as well, or you will lose marks. Here is a sample writing task from SQA.

> Éric nous a parlé de son attitude envers les matières qu'il a choisies au lycée. Et vous, qu'est-ce qui vous a influencé(e) dans votre choix de matières? Pensez-vous que vous avez fait un bon choix? Pensez-vous que le cours que vous suivez maintenant va vous être utile à l'avenir?
>
> Écrivez 120–150 mots pour exprimer vos idées.

You are asked to talk about what you are doing at school and about what you will do in the future, which is quite straightforward, and allows you to introduce material you will know well. However, there are a couple of things you have to watch: first, don't just give a list of your subjects, as lists are as bad at Higher as they are at Standard Grade. Second, your answers to the questions should include reasons and opinions, as this is a personal response.

So you might start off with something like this:

> Cette année au lycée j'ai choisi cinq matières. Je fais l'anglais, bien sûr, parce que c'est nécessaire pour l'université. Je fais aussi les maths, parce que mes parents trouvent ça essentiel. En plus, j'ai choisi la biologie, car le prof est vraiment sympa.

This is about one-third of the total necessary, and, although it is very simple and straightforward, it does answer the first question. The next question is about you having made the right choice. Try to choose one subject you are happy with and one that you are not: that allows you to give different opinions. Then you could continue:

> Je regrette d'avoir choisi les maths, je trouve ça trop difficile et j'ai peur de ne pas réussir à mon Higher de maths. Mais je suis très contente d'avoir choisi le Français, j'ai appris beaucoup cette année.

This now leads you to the final question, about your future plans. All you have to say here is what you intend to do, and remember to link this in some way to what you are doing just now.

> J'ai décidé que j'irai en fac l'année prochaine pour faire des études. Je voudrais étudier la biologie, parce que je m'y intéresse beaucoup, mais je pense que mon Français me sera utile, parce que je pourrai faire un stage Erasmus.

This answer is not complex, but has a variety of tenses and structures in it. It is not quite long enough, but you can put in other material which you have prepared, as it does answer all the questions. Learn some really good material, use it appropriately, and keep things simple when answering the specific questions, as these are likely to bring in some areas you have to make up on the spot.

Preparing for the paper

So how can you prepare best for this paper? The answer is to have a bank of material on each of the main topic areas. This could well include the material you prepared for your Speaking assessment, so look at Chapter 10 (Speaking) for some ideas. Look also at the textbook or texts you are working from for good ideas you can use, and find a good place to store these. This might be a part of your folder, a special exercise book, or on your computer. Some more things you should do are:

◆ go to Chapter 14 (Structures and vocabulary) for ideas;

◆ prepare different ways of giving your opinion, and work at having different ways of saying what you think;

◆ make sure you have a variety of tenses in each of the areas;

◆ have a variety of adjectives and adverbs for opinions, not just *bien* or *difficile*;

◆ have a couple of really impressive bits for each topic area, which you can put in whatever the question; and

◆ share your work with your teacher, to get any suggestions or corrections made.

To help you prepare for a writing assessment, we have included a Personal Response task with each of the Listening assessments in Chapter 6 (Listening): you should look at these, and see how you would go about answering the specific questions in French. Try some of them and ask your teacher if they could mark them for you.

Chapter 13

UNIT WRITING

You will have to carry out four Unit assessments or NABs for your Higher French. Reading, listening and speaking are assessed through the Language Unit, but writing is assessed through the Optional Unit, that is, either Extended Reading and Viewing, or Language in Work.

For Extended Reading and Viewing, you will have to produce a written personal response in French to the text or texts you have studied. This response should be 100–150 words long.

For Language in Work, you will have to produce a folio of three pieces of practical writing, two letters (of 100–150 words each) and an email message (of 50–80 words).

For both units, you will have to produce the piece of work to be assessed under controlled conditions, that is, in class under supervision – what are often called 'exam conditions'. For both units, the assessment is a simple pass/fail style.

Extended Reading and Viewing

There is no set text for Extended Reading and Viewing, and each school and teacher will have their own favourites, or will decide together with you what you are going to study. The subject of the writing for Extended Reading and Viewing will be set by your teacher in discussion with you, and you can draft and redraft, following advice from your teacher. Just as at Standard Grade, you can use the text or texts you are studying, and work you have already produced, to guide you in your preparation.

The criteria you will be assessed by are as set out below.

> **Performance criteria**
> (a) Provides appropriately organised information relevant to the area of study.
> (b) Employs appropriate language with a reasonable degree of accuracy as appropriate to this level.
> (c) Demonstrates ability to use some variety of vocabulary and structures.

Once you have produced a good draft, you will have to reproduce it on the day of the assessment. This is similar to what you have to do with a presentation at Intermediate 2 or Higher, or with a solo talk or writing assessment at Standard Grade.

Language in Work

The subjects of the letters and message for Language in Work will come from four areas:
◆ work experience
◆ business studies

HOW TO PASS HIGHER FRENCH

◆ travel and tourism

◆ information technology.

The letters will be based upon a stimulus task **in French**, which will set the context and give you a number (6 or 7) of bullet points to address. Make sure you tick off all the bullet points! For email, you will be given a similar task to the letters but you will only be asked to give a few details, and will not need all the introductory and concluding phrases. You do not have to do them both on the same day, or even in the same week! You can prepare drafts of these, and show them to your teacher for advice before redrafting. Both letter and message must be written under controlled conditions finally. However, you are entitled to use model letters and messages on which to base your answer, when you are writing your first drafts, as well as a dictionary during the actual assessment. Most dictionaries will have the formal beginnings and endings of letters for you to copy – you should not have to learn these off by heart! The criteria you will be assessed by are very similar to those for Extended Reading and Viewing, but require a high level of accuracy, to reflect the nature of the task and the additional support provided by having a model.

Performance criteria

(a) Provides appropriately organised information relevant to the format.

This means using appropriate information, structuring it well, giving all the information asked for, and using stock phrases correctly.

(b) Employs appropriate language with a high degree of accuracy appropriate to this level.

This means using the correct register, using formal language, and having a good level of accuracy in spelling and grammar.

(c) Demonstrates ability to use some variety of vocabulary and structure if appropriate to the task.

This means using a range of structures and vocabulary, and having some complex sentences.

Planning your writing

Try to follow these guidelines to make it easier for yourself:

◆ start in plenty of time, to allow time for redrafting and learning;

◆ show your teacher a draft early on;

◆ try to use a computer, to make it easier to redraft;

◆ remember you need a variety of vocabulary and structure;

◆ for Extended Reading and Viewing, remember your opinion is what matters; and

◆ for Language in Work, remember accuracy of spelling and grammar is crucial.

Carrying out your writing

Remember to do the following:

◆ Look at your own learning style: how do you remember things best? You should do the same as you do for your presentation, and prepare in the same way.

◆ Practise proofreading, particularly for Language in Work, where it is vital.

◆ Use your dictionary to check your spelling and verb endings, not to look up new words!

◆ Remember to find where the stock phrases are in your dictionary when it comes to the Language in Work letters.

STRUCTURES AND VOCABULARY

For your Higher French, you will have to produce a variety of pieces of work in French. For speaking, these are the Presentation and Discussion, and for writing, the Directed Writing as well as the Personal Response Writing, along with the work you produce for the Optional Unit. You will be assessed in both skills on, among other things, your use of structure, your ability to give opinions and reasons, and the accurate use of a variety of grammatical structures and vocabulary.

Structure

This means that your work should be directly related to the topic you are writing or speaking about. You will lose marks for work which is disorganised or irrelevant to the question set.

◆ For your Presentation, as well as for the Personal Response, that means using a structure where you introduce the topic, give your information and your opinions, and come to a conclusion.

◆ For the Directed Writing it means following the bullet points, and addressing each of the points adequately.

◆ For Language in Work, it means following closely the template or model from which you are working.

Giving opinions and reasons

Giving opinions is crucial to any personal response, and also to any presentation or follow-up discussion. It is worth mastering all the vocabulary you learned for Standard Grade or Intermediate 2, so that it comes easily to you and you don't have to think about it: make sure you have a variety of phrases, and do not just stick to your favourite three or four. To remind you, here is what you should know already:

J'aime, J'adore, Je préfère	I like, I love, I prefer
Je n'aime pas, Je déteste	I don't like, I hate
J'ai horreur de …	I really hate …
Je trouve que c'est …	I think that it's …
Je trouve cela formidable	I find that terrific
Je trouve bête que …	I find it stupid that …
C'est fantastique, très bien, génial	That's fantastic, very good, great
intéressant, passionnant, marrant	interesting, exciting, fun
C'est minable, triste, déprimant	That's awful, sad, depressing
pénible, nul, ennuyeux	terrible, no good, boring
Il est mieux/pire de …	It is better/worse to …
Il y a trop de … (Il y avait …)	There is/are too much/many … (There were …)
Il n'y a pas assez de …	There is/are not enough …
Il serait utile de pouvoir …	It would be useful to be able to …

À mon avis		In my opinion
Il faut penser à …		You have to think about …
Il ne faut pas oublier que …		We mustn't forget that …
Nous devons … Nous ne devons pas …		We should … We shouldn't …
J'aimerais savoir que …		I would like to know that …
Je voudrais voir …		I would like to see …

However, for Higher, you need to do more with these. You need to start giving reasons for your opinions. When answering a question in the discussion on whether you are interested in sport, it is not enough to say:

Non, je n'aime pas le sport.

You have to build on this, and say something like:

Non, je n'aime pas le sport, car je trouve bête qu'on doive sortir sous la pluie pour participer à une activité que je ne supporte pas.

This leads us on to the next part, conjunctions: get into the habit of giving a reason when you give an opinion, and get into the habit of using conjunctions all the time. It will make your writing or speaking flow better, which means better structured work and a higher mark.

Using conjunctions

Giving reasons for your opinions can be done by simply stating the reason. However, it is much better for your work to use a conjunction, as this allows you to use more complex grammatical structures. How many do you know? Start off with these, add more as you come across them, and start using them. Look at the sentences below and try to work out what they mean.

mais	but	J'aime bien le sport, mais je ne suis pas fanatique.
car	because	J'adore ma sœur, car je peux lui parler de tout.
parce que	because	Je trouve ça nul, parce que c'est très difficile et ça m'embête.
comme	as	Comme il pleut, je ne veux pas sortir.
donc	so	Je trouve ça minable, donc je préfère ne pas y aller.
par conséquent	therefore	J'ai trouvé la géo très difficile, par conséquent je n'en fais plus.
quand	when	J'allais sortir, quand ma mère m'a persuadé de rester.
lorsque	when	Lorsque j'étais plus jeune, j'aimais Kylie, mais maintenant, je ne la supporte plus.
pendant que	while	Pendant que je serai en vacances, je voudrais rester en forme.
comment	how	Je ne comprends pas comment je peux faire plus d'effort.
si	if	Je ne demande si je l'aime ou non.
ce que	what	Ce que je n'aime pas, c'est la violence dans la rue.

Grammatical structures

Your grade at Higher (and even your pass/fail) will depend upon your accuracy with these. The grammar grid in Appendix Two gives an overview of what you should know, but here briefly are the main things you should be doing. If you do not understand any of them, find out what they mean! You should be

- getting the gender and plural form of your nouns right;
- attaching adjectives to nouns with the correct endings and in the correct place;
- using comparatives;
- using a variety of negatives with your verbs;
- using pronouns correctly: that means the correct form, the correct gender and in the correct place;
- using reflexive pronouns (and reflexive verbs) correctly; and
- using prepositions correctly.

And of course knowing about verbs is the single most important thing you can do! You need to get those endings right, which means learning them, but also knowing how to check them in a dictionary, as French has quite a few irregular verbs which do not follow the normal pattern. Here are the tenses you should know and understand: it is your job to match these up with the correct endings!

The present

The present tense only has one form, unlike in English. Make sure you do not try to translate 'I am working at home' word for word: this is *Je travaille à la maison*. Equally, 'When do you go?' does not need the word *fais* in French.

The past

You should be able to use at least three tenses in the past: these tenses have various names, although most books refer to them as the perfect, the pluperfect and the imperfect. You should use the perfect to talk about a single event in the past, and the imperfect to describe how things were, used to be or often were.

Je suis parti à six heures du matin.

Il faisait mauvais.

J'allais souvent au cinéma quand j'étais plus jeune.

The pluperfect is used in complex sentences when one thing happened before the other:

I had already eaten when he arrived.
J'avais déjà mangé lorsqu'il est arrivé.

You might also come across a verb tense called the 'past historic' or *passé simple*. You do not have to be able to use this for Higher, but many of the texts you read will feature it.

The future and conditional

You should be able to use the informal future, the formal future and the conditional.

On va visiter la France cet été.

J'irai avec mes copines.

J'aimerais aller à Paris,

The subjunctive

You should be able to recognise the subjunctive, and use it at some points in your writing. It may sound difficult, but a French toddler who needs to go urgently will shout out '*Il faut que j'aille*', so if a French two-year-old can use the subjunctive, so can you! You will find some examples of this in Chapter 10 (Speaking).

Vocabulary

The vocabulary you will need is the vocabulary you work on as you go through the course, so make sure you keep a note of it in a way which makes sense to you. That might be in a vocabulary book, in spidergrams, or in a folder divided into topics. However, listed here are some adjectives and adverbs, as well as some basics from Standard Grade for you to revise from, as it will be assumed that you know them. These include numbers: it is amazing how many people cannot remember them during the Listening assessments!

Adjectives

Adjectives are useful for giving opinions, and for improving the quality of your speaking and writing. Here are a few to work from, but add your own as you come across them. If you do not know them, look them up!

affreux		extraordinaire		pénible	
agréable		gênant		pratique	
autoritaire		génial		préféré	
barbant		impressionnant		raisonnable	
bizarre		magnifique		rigolo	
cher, pas cher		malade		sain	
choquant		modeste		sale	
chouette		nul		sensible	
cool		ouvert		seul	
démodé		parfait		sévère	
désagréable		pas mal		strict	
embêtant		passionnant		sympa	
ennuyeux		patient		vieux	

Adverbs

Adverbs describe and modify verbs, but they are also very useful with adjectives, to make your language seem more natural: *C'est absolument nul! Je le trouve légèrement ennuyeux.*

Get into the habit of using them: here are a few to start with.

absolument		jamais	
assez		même	
bien		un peu	
en général		totalement	
extrêmement		toujours	
fortement		très	
légèrement		trop	

Times

neuf heures	nine o'clock
neuf heures et quart	quarter past nine
neuf heures vingt	twenty past nine
neuf heures et demie	half past nine
neuf heures moins le quart	quarter to nine
neuf heures moins cinq	five to nine
midi et demi, minuit et demi	half past twelve

Remember that most official times in French will use the 24-hour clock, and there is no use of a.m. and p.m.

treize heures	1 p.m.
dix-huit heures trente	6.30 p.m.
le matin	morning
l'après-midi	afternoon
le soir	evening
la nuit	night

Seasons

le printemps
l'été
l'automne
l'hiver

Dates and time expressions

mercredi 25 novembre	Wednesday 25 November
Je suis né le 14 octobre	I was born on 14 October
une semaine	a week
quinze jours	a fortnight
un mois	a month
un an	a year (used with a number)
J'ai quinze ans	I am 15
une année	a year (used with an adjective)

| une bonne année | a good year |
| mille neuf cent quatre-vingt treize | 1993 |

Measurements and prices

Remember that you should never use measurements like miles when talking and writing in French, but always metres and kilometres.

Glasgow se trouve à 80 kilomètres d'Édimbourg.

J'habite à 500 mètres de l'école.

Prices are all in euros and cents: old prices in francs are still in some books, but they will not feature in your exam.

Un Coca coûte 3 euros. J'ai payé 3,50€.

When writing about yourself, you should use *livre* for pounds.

Je gagne 20 livres tous les samedis au magasin.

The weather

la météo	the weather forecast
Quel temps fait-il?	What is the weather like?
Il fait beau tous les jours	The weather is fine every day
Il y a du soleil de temps en temps	It is sunny now and then
Il fait chaud (Il ne fait jamais chaud)	It is hot (It's never hot)
La température est de 25 degrés	It is 25° centigrade
Il fait souvent mauvais	The weather is often bad
Il fait froid en hiver	It is cold in winter
Il gèle pendant la nuit	It freezes over at night
Il y a du vent assez souvent	It is quite often windy
Il y a du brouillard en automne	It is foggy in autumn
Il pleut maintenant	It is raining now
Il neige en hiver	It snows in winter
Il y a de la tempête	It is stormy

Jobs and professions

Remember that, when talking about what a person does, you do not need *une*: *Mon père est dentiste*.

acteur/actrice	actor/actress
agent de police	policeman/woman
agriculteur	farmer
avocat	lawyer
boucher/bouchère	butcher
boulanger/boulangère	baker
caissier/caissière	cashier
chauffeur de taxi	taxi driver
chômeur/chômeuse	unemployed person
coiffeur/coiffeuse	hairdresser
cuisinier/cuisinière	cook
directeur/directrice	headteacher, director

dentiste	dentist
électricien/électricienne	electrician
facteur/factrice	postman/woman
hôtesse de l'air	air stewardess
jardinier/jardinière	gardener
journaliste	journalist
infirmier/infirmière	nurse
ingénieur	engineer
maçon	bricklayer, builder
mécanicien/mécanicienne	mechanic
médecin	doctor
patron/patronne	boss, owner
plombier/plombière	plumber
PDG	managing director
professeur	teacher
secrétaire	secretary
serveur/serveuse	waiter/waitress, barman
technicien/technicienne	technician
vendeur/vendeuse	shop/sales assistant

Starter sentences

Ma mère est professeur	My mum is a teacher
Je voudrais devenir infirmière	I'd like to be a nurse
Je vais aller en fac	I'm going to go to university
Je veux continuer mes études	I'm going to stay on at school
Le samedi, je travaille dans un café	I work in a café on Saturdays
J'ai un petit boulot comme vendeuse	I have a part-time job in a shop

School subjects

l'allemand (m)	German
l'anglais (m)	English
la biologie	biology
la chimie	chemistry
le commerce	business management
le dessin	art
l'EMT (m)	craft and design
l'EPS (f)	PE
l'espagnol	Spanish
le français	French
la géographie	geography
l'histoire (f)	history
l'informatique (f)	IT
les maths (fpl)	maths
la musique	music
la politique/l'instruction civique (f)	modern studies
la physique	physics
les sciences nat (fpl)	science
le sport	sport
la technologie	technological studies

School (general)

le collège/CES	secondary school (S1–4)
le lycée	secondary school (S5/6)
le bac/baccalauréat	equivalent to Highers
une bibliothèque	library
un bulletin	report
une cantine	canteen
un cours	lesson
les devoirs (mpl)	homework
un/une élève	pupil
les études (fpl)	study, schoolwork
un examen	exam
la fac/l'université (f)	uni/university
un laboratoire	laboratory
une matière	a subject
la pause de midi	lunchtime
un/une professeur	teacher
la récréation/la récré	morning interval, break
une salle de classe	classroom
les vacances (fpl)	holidays
les grandes vacances	summer holidays
les vacances de Pâques, de Noël	Easter, Christmas holidays

Remember that French pupils refer to the fifth year as *seconde* and use *terminale* for the last year in school. The equivalent of Highers is the *bac*.

Starter sentences

Je vais passer mes examens en mai	I'm going to sit my exams in May
J'espère réussir à mes examens	I hope to pass my exams
J'ai reçu de bonnes notes en …	I got good marks in …
Ma matière préférée est le Français	My favourite subject is French
Ce que je n'aime pas du tout, c'est …	What I really don't like is …
Je pense que le prof est moche	I think the teacher is awful
Je trouve que j'ai trop de devoirs	I have too much homework, I think
L'année prochaine, je vais continuer mes études au lycée	I'm staying on next year

Family members

la famille	family
les parents	parents
le père	father
la mère	mother
le mari	husband
la femme	wife
le frère, mon frère aîné/cadet	brother, my older/younger brother
la sœur, ma sœur aînée/cadette	sister, my older/younger sister
le fils	son
la fille	daughter
un jumeau/une jumelle	twin

HOW TO PASS HIGHER FRENCH

le grand-père	grandfather
la grand-mère	grandmother
les grands-parents	grandparents
un petit-fils/une petite-fille/les petits-enfants	grandson/granddaughter/grandchildren
un oncle	uncle
une tante	aunt
un cousin/une cousine	cousin
un neveu	nephew
une nièce	niece

Starter sentences

Nous sommes quatre dans ma famille	There are four of us
Je n'ai pas de frères/sœurs/Je suis enfant unique	I don't have any brothers/sisters
J'ai une sœur et deux frères	I have a sister and two brothers
Mon frère/ma sœur s'appelle …	My brother/sister is called …
Mes parents s'appellent …	My parents are called …
Mes parents sont séparés/divorcés	My parents are separated/divorced
Je m'entends bien avec mes parents	I get on well with my parents
Mes parents sont très sympa	My parents are very nice
Quelquefois, je me dispute avec ma mère	I sometimes have arguments with my mum
Ma sœur est très gentille	My sister is very nice
Je peux discuter de mes problèmes avec …	I can talk about my problems with …
Je ne m'entends pas bien avec mon frère	I don't get on well with my brother
Mon frère m'énerve	My brother gets on my nerves

Hobbies and sports

Je vais au cinéma	I go to the cinema
Je vais à la pêche	I go fishing
J'écoute de la musique	I listen to music
Je lis des magazines/des livres	I read magazines/books
Je regarde la télé/les DVD	I watch TV/DVDs
Je fais du patin	I go ice-skating
Je fais du roller	I go rollerblading
Je fais du cyclisme/du vélo	I go on my bike
Je fais du VTT	I go mountain biking
Je fais du skateboard	I go boarding
Je fais de l'équitation	I go horse-riding
Je fais de la gymnastique	I do gymnastics
Je fais de la natation/Je nage	I go swimming
Je fais du ski	I go skiing
Je fais du sport	I do sport
Je fais de la voile	I go sailing
Je joue aux jeux vidéo	I play video games
Je joue avec l'ordinateur	I play on the computer
Je joue **de la** guitare/**du** piano	I play (for a musical instrument)
Je joue **au** basket, **au** foot, **au** rugby	I play (for a team sport)

Starter sentences

Il y a beaucoup de choses à faire à Glasgow	There is lots to do in Glasgow
Il n'y a rien à faire pour les jeunes	There is nothing for young people
Il n'y a pas beaucoup ici	There is not a lot here
Il n'y a pas de cinéma	There is no cinema
On peut aller à la maison des jeunes	You can go to the youth club
Je joue au foot tous les week-ends	I play football every weekend
Je vais au cinéma avec mes copains	I go to the cinema with my friends
Mon sport préféré, c'est le …	My favourite sport is …
Moi, j'adore jouer au tennis	I really love playing tennis
Ce que je ne supporte pas, c'est le …	What I really can't stand is …
Le mardi, je joue au hockey: c'est génial!	I play hockey on Tuesdays: it's brilliant!
Je suis membre d'un club de golf	I belong to a golf club
Je suis membre de l'équipe de hockey	I'm in the hockey team

House, daily routine and household tasks

un appartement	flat
la cave	cellar
la chambre	bedroom
la cuisine	kitchen
la douche	shower
un étage	floor (first, second, and so on)
un grenier	attic
un immeuble	block of flats
la maison	house
la salle à manger	dining room
la salle de bains	bathroom
le séjour	living room
Je me réveille à …	I wake up at …
Je me lève	I get up
Je me lave	I get washed
Je m'habille	I get dressed
Je prends mon petit déjeuner/déjeuner/dîner	I have my breakfast, etc.
Je quitte la maison	I leave the house
Je prends le bus	I get the bus
Je rentre à la maison	I get home
Je me couche	I go to bed
Je fais les courses	I do the shopping
J'aide ma mère à …	I help my mum to …
Je m'occupe de mon frère	I look after my brother
Je fais du babysitting	I babysit
Je fais la cuisine	I do the cooking
Je prépare le dîner	I make the tea
Je fais du jardinage	I work in the garden
Je tonds le gazon	I cut the grass
Je fais mon lit	I make my bed
Je fais la vaisselle	I do the washing-up
Je fais la lessive	I do the washing

Je lave la voiture	I wash the car
Je mets la table	I set the table
Je range/je débarrasse la table	I clear the table
Je passe l'aspirateur	I do the hoovering
Je range ma chambre	I tidy my room
Je sors la poubelle	I take out the rubbish

Starter sentences

Souvent je dois faire les courses pour ma mère	I often have to do the messages for mum
De temps en temps, il me faut ranger ma chambre	Sometimes I have to tidy my room
Tous les jours, je fais mon lit: quelle barbe!	I make my bed every day: how boring!
Je ne fais jamais la lessive	I never do the washing

Places in town

un aéroport	an airport
un arrêt d'autobus	bus stop
la banque	bank
le bâtiment	building
la bibliothèque	library
la boîte	nightclub
le camping	campsite
le centre commercial	shopping centre
le centre sportif	sports complex
le château	castle
le cinéma	cinema
la cité	housing estate
le collège/l'école	school
le commissariat/la gendarmerie	police station
une église	church
la gare	station
la gare routière	bus station
un grand magasin	department store
un hôpital	hospital
un hôtel de ville	town hall
le magasin	shop
la mairie	town hall
le marché	market
la maison des jeunes	youth club
le métro	underground
un monument	monument/tourist sight
le musée	museum
le parc	park
la patinoire	skating rink
la piscine	swimming pool
la place	square
le pont	bridge
le port	harbour, port
la poste/PTT	post office

le stade	stadium
la station-service	petrol station
le syndicat d'initiative	tourist information
le théâtre	theatre
la zone piétonne	pedestrian precinct

Starter sentences

À Perth, il y a beaucoup à faire et à voir!	There's lots to do and see in Perth!
Il n'y a pas beaucoup de chose pour les jeunes	There's not a lot for young people
Chez nous, il y a une piscine	We have a swimming pool
On n'a pas de gare	We don't have a station
J'habite Dumfries depuis douze ans	I've lived in Dumfries for twelve years

Methods of transport

en auto/voiture	by car
en autobus/car	by bus
en avion	by plane
en bateau	by boat
en métro	by underground
à moto	by motorbike
à pied	on foot
en train	by train
à vélo	by bike

Starter sentences

Je vais au collège à pied, normalement	Usually I walk to school
Nous sommes allés en bus ...	We went by bus to ...
Quand il pleut, je prends le bus	I go by bus when it's raining
Je préfère y aller en voiture, c'est plus rapide	I prefer going by car, it's quicker
Nous sommes allés en France en train	We went to France by train
Je préfère y aller à vélo, c'est plus facile	I prefer to go by bike, it's easier

APPENDIX ONE: THEMES AND TOPICS

This table is taken from the SQA (Scottish Qualifications Authority) website and, as such, is a valuable resource. You should use it to assist in your preparation work and revision.

Language Unit

Themes	Topics	Topic development
Lifestyles	Family, friends, society	◆ issues in relationships with friends/family ◆ role of the individual in the home and in society ◆ advantages/disadvantages of home area
	Leisure and healthy living	◆ leisure interests ◆ health issues
Education and work	School/college	◆ critique of own school/college ◆ personal achievement to date such as in a record of achievement or an ELP*
	Careers	◆ job intentions and aspirations ◆ employment issues
The wider world	Holidays and travel	◆ comparison of types of holiday/travel ◆ past holidays/journeys
	Tourism	◆ critique of local area in Scotland as tourist centre ◆ areas of interest in target-language country/countries and beyond

*European Languages Passport (Council of Europe, 2001)

Verbs

	Access	Intermediate 1	Intermediate 2	Higher	Advanced Higher
Person	The person involved is indicated clearly by pronoun/noun. Meaning of the verb is clear.	Notion of endings of verbs for regular verbs and common irregular verbs. Person must be clear from the verb if the language does not usually use pronouns.		Less common irregular verbs. →→	
Time	Notion of time may be unclear from the verb. Other time words may make timing obvious.	Notion of present, future and past time clear from verb (though may be very inaccurate in form). Increasing accuracy of form in regular and then common and less common irregular verbs.	Generally recognisable forms of: ◆ present ◆ immediate future (or future) ◆ completed past ◆ continuous past	Future →→ Pluperfect (or equivalent) →	Other past tenses
Mood/ modality	Notions of volition (would like to ...); being able to; imperatives (must do something ...) as learned in common phrases.	Some manipulation of verbal forms. →	Control of modal verbs in common tenses. (Verbs) expressing beliefs, opinions. Conditional tense or equivalent.	- - - (Verbs) expressing feelings, hopes. - - - - Reporting others' (if relevant) views, speech.	Modals in less common tenses. → Subjunctive forms.
Commands	Common singular/ plural commands.	Command rules for common irregular/ regular verbs.			

Nouns

	Access	Intermediate 1	Intermediate 2	Higher	Advanced Higher
Gender		Notion of gender; most common words remembered.	Some conventions of gender, individual nouns showing increasing accuracy.	→	
Number		Singular/plural indicated by noun, or article or number or ending for common words.	Common irregular plurals.	Rules of plural forms. →	
Case		If relevant, case made evident enough to give clear meaning by the noun or article as necessary. ‹- - - - - -›	Concept of case shown by noun or modifier as appropriate. →		

Pronouns

	Access	Intermediate 1	Intermediate 2	Higher	Advanced Higher
Subject/ Object		(See person of verb above.) If relevant, able to distinguish I/you/we/one as subject or object.	Subject and direct object pronouns (all).	Indirect object pronouns (as relevant in the language). →	
Reflexive		Common reflexive verbal forms with pronouns as learned phrases. ‹- - - - - -›	Reflexives with common verbs in appropriate tenses. →		

	Access	Intermediate 1	Intermediate 2	Higher	Advanced Higher
Emphatic	First/second person.	→	All persons.		→
Relative				Common relative pronouns, in different cases as relevant.	Less common relative pronouns.
Position		Notion of position of direct or indirect pronouns (NB: commands).	Notion of rules where more than one pronoun is involved.	→	

Adjectives

	Access	Intermediate 1	Intermediate 2	Higher	Advanced Higher
Rules of agreement		Notion of agreement and common forms – regular plus some irregular.	Increasing irregular forms or ending rules for case as relevant.	→	
Rules of position		Notion of position of adjectives.	Rules of position.	→	
Possessives	My/Your.	Indication of possessive for all persons.	Agreements as appropriate.	→	
Comparative/ Superlative	Indication of comparative.	→	Common irregular comparatives. Notion of superlatives.	Less common comparatives and superlatives.	

Adverbs

	Access	Intermediate 1	Intermediate 2	Higher	Advanced Higher
Rules of order			Notion (where relevant) of rules of order. →		
Comparative/ Superlative		Indication of comparative. →	Common irregular comparatives. Notion of superlatives.	Less common comparatives and superlatives. →	

Prepositions

	Access	Intermediate 1	Intermediate 2	Higher	Advanced Higher
		Notion that prepositions may change case/form of noun/article, etc., as relevant. →	Most common prepositional effects. →	Less common prepositional effects. →	

Other

Key concepts of grammatical features of any language not definable by the foregoing categories should be handled in similar ways in a continuum through Intermediate 1 to Advanced Higher, as appropriate. →

APPENDIX THREE: SUMMARY OF ASSESSMENT PROCEDURES

Internal

UNIT Language	Speaking	Presentation on topic of choice; follow-up discussion
	Listening	1 text 2–3 minutes; responses in English; played up to 3 times
	Reading	1 text 400–450 words
UNIT Extended Reading/ Viewing	Option A Writing	**Extended Reading/Viewing** Written personal response to aspect of text(s) studied (100–150 words) in target language
UNIT Language in Work	Option B Writing	**Language in Work** Practical writing (2 letters 150–180 words and 1 email 50–80 words) in target language

External

Speaking	25%	As for the Language Unit, marked out of 25
Listening	20%	1 text 2–3 minutes, interview, played twice (20 minutes approximately)
Reading	30%	1 text 550–650 words (55 minutes), including translation into English
Writing	25%	Personal opinion 120–150 words, linked to Listening (40 minutes approximately) Directed writing to stimulus in English 150–180 words (45 minutes approximately)

APPENDIX FOUR: DIRECTED WRITING

Category	Mark	Content	Accuracy	Language Resource – Variety, Range, Structures
Very Good	15	◆ All bullet points are covered fully, in a balanced way, including a number of complex sentences. ◆ Some candidates may also provide additional information. ◆ A wide range of verbs/verb forms, tenses and construction is used. ◆ Overall this comes as a competent, well thought-out account of the event which reads naturally.	◆ The candidate handles all aspects of grammar and spelling accurately, although the language may contain some minor errors or even one more serious error. ◆ Where the candidate attempts to use language more appropriate to post-Higher, a slightly higher number of inaccuracies need not detract from the overall very good impression.	◆ The candidate is comfortable with almost all the grammar used and generally uses a different verb or verb form in each sentence. ◆ There is good use of a variety of tenses, adjectives, adverbs and prepositional phrases and, where appropriate, word order. ◆ The candidate uses co-ordinating conjunctions and subordinate clauses throughout the writing. ◆ The language flows well.
Good	12	◆ All bullet points are addressed, generally quite fully, and some complex sentences may be included. ◆ The response to one bullet point may be thin, although other bullet points are dealt with in some detail. ◆ The candidate uses a reasonable range of verbs/verb forms and other constructions.	◆ The candidate generally handles verbs and other parts of speech accurately but simply. ◆ There may be some errors in spelling, adjective endings and, where relevant, case endings. ◆ Use of accents may be less secure. ◆ Where the candidate is attempting to use more complex vocabulary and structures, these may be less successful, although basic structures are used accurately. ◆ There may be minor misuse of dictionary.	◆ There may be less variety in the verbs used. ◆ Most of the more complex sentences use co-ordinating conjunctions, and there may also be examples of subordinating conjunctions where appropriate. ◆ In one bullet point the language may be more basic than might otherwise be expected at this level. ◆ Overall the writing will be competent, mainly correct, but pedestrian.

Category	Mark	Content	Accuracy	Language Resource – Variety, Range, Structures
Satisfactory	9	◆ The candidate uses mainly simple, more basic sentences. ◆ The language is perhaps repetitive and uses a limited range of verbs and fixed phrases not appropriate to this level. ◆ In some examples, one or two bullet points may be less fully addressed. ◆ In some cases, the content may be similar to that of good or very good examples, but with some serious accuracy issues.	◆ The verbs are generally correct, but basic. ◆ Tenses may be inconsistent, with present tenses being used at times instead of past tenses. ◆ There are quite a few errors in other parts of speech – personal pronouns, gender of nouns, adjective endings, cases, singular/plural confusion – and in the use of accents. ◆ Some prepositions may be inaccurate or omitted e.g. I went the town. ◆ While the language may be reasonably accurate in three or four bullet points, in the remaining two control of the language structure may deteriorate significantly. ◆ Overall, there is more correct than incorrect and there is the impression overall that the candidate can handle tenses.	◆ The candidate copes with the past tense of some verbs. ◆ A limited range of verbs is used to address some of the bullet points. ◆ Candidate relies on a limited range of vocabulary and structures. ◆ When using the perfect tense, the past participle is incorrect or the auxiliary verb is omitted on occasion. ◆ Sentences may be basic and mainly brief. ◆ There is minimal use of adjectives, probably mainly after 'is' e.g. The boss was helpful. ◆ The candidate has a weak knowledge of plurals. ◆ There may be several spelling errors e.g. reversal of vowel combinations.

Category	Mark	Content	Accuracy	Language Resource – Variety, Range, Structures
Unsatisfactory	6	◆ In some cases the content may be basic. ◆ In other cases there may be little difference in content between Satisfactory and Unsatisfactory. ◆ The language is repetitive, with undue reliance on fixed phrases and a limited range of common basic verbs such as *to be, to have, to play, to watch*. ◆ While the language used to address the more predictable bullet points may be accurate, serious errors occur when the candidate attempts to address the less predictable areas. ◆ The Directed Writing may be presented as a single paragraph.	◆ Ability to form tenses is inconsistent. ◆ In the use of the perfect tense the auxiliary verb is omitted on a number of occasions. ◆ There may be confusion between the singular and plural form of verbs. ◆ There are errors in many other parts of speech – gender of nouns, cases, singular/plural confusion – and in spelling and, where appropriate, word order. ◆ Several errors are serious, perhaps showing mother tongue interference. ◆ There may be one sentence which is not intelligible to a sympathetic native speaker. ◆ One area may be very weak. ◆ Overall, there is more incorrect than correct.	◆ The candidate copes mainly only with the predictable language required at the earlier bullet points. ◆ The verbs 'was' and 'went' may also be used correctly. ◆ There is inconsistency in the use of various expressions, especially verbs. ◆ Sentences are more basic. ◆ An English word may appear in the writing or a word may be omitted. ◆ There may be an example of serious dictionary misuse.

Category	Mark	Content	Accuracy	Language Resource – Variety, Range, Structures
Poor	3	◆ The content and language may be very basic. ◆ However, in many cases the content may be little different from that expected at Unsatisfactory or even at Satisfactory.	◆ Many of the verbs are incorrect or even omitted. ◆ There are many errors in other parts of speech – personal pronouns, gender of nouns, adjective endings, cases, singular/plural confusion – and in spelling and word order. ◆ Prepositions are not used correctly. ◆ The language is probably inaccurate throughout the writing. ◆ Some sentences may not be understood by a sympathetic native speaker.	◆ The candidate cannot cope with more than one or two basic verbs, frequently 'had' and 'was'. ◆ The candidate displays almost no knowledge of past tenses of verbs. ◆ Verbs used more than once may be written differently on each occasion. ◆ The candidate has a very limited vocabulary. ◆ Several English or 'made-up' words may appear in the writing. ◆ There are examples of serious dictionary misuse.
Very Poor	0	◆ The content is very basic OR ◆ The candidate has not completed at least three of the core bullet points.	◆ (Virtually) nothing is correct. ◆ Most of the errors are serious. ◆ Very little is intelligible to a sympathetic native speaker.	◆ The candidate copes only with 'have' and 'am'. ◆ Very few words are correctly written in the foreign language. ◆ English words are used. ◆ There may be several examples of mother tongue interference. ◆ There may be several examples of serious dictionary misuse.

Category	Mark	Content	Accuracy	Language Resource – Variety, Range, Structures
Very Good	10	◆ The topic is covered fully, in a balanced way, including a number of complex sentences. Some candidates may also provide additional information. ◆ A wide range of verbs/verb forms and constructions is used. There may also be a variety of tenses. ◆ Overall this comes over as a competent, well thought-out response to the task which reads naturally.	◆ The candidate handles all aspects of grammar and spelling accurately, although the language may contain some minor errors or even one more serious error. ◆ Where the candidate attempts to use language more appropriate to post-Higher, a slightly higher number of inaccuracies need not detract from the overall very good impression.	◆ The candidate is comfortable with almost all the grammar used and generally uses a different verb or verb form in each sentence. ◆ There is good use of a variety of tenses, adjectives, adverbs and prepositional phrases and, where appropriate, word order. ◆ The candidate uses co-ordinating conjunctions and subordinate clauses throughout the writing. ◆ The language flows well.
Good	8	◆ The topic is addressed, generally quite fully, and some complex sentences may be included. ◆ The candidate uses a reasonable range of verbs/verb forms and other constructions.	◆ The candidate generally handles verbs and other parts of speech accurately but simply. ◆ There may be some errors in spelling, adjective endings and, where relevant, case endings. ◆ Use of accents may be less secure. ◆ Where the candidate is attempting to use more complex vocabulary and structures, these may be less successful, although basic structures are used accurately. ◆ There may be minor misuse of dictionary.	◆ There may be less variety in the verbs used. ◆ Most of the more complex sentences use co-ordinating conjunctions, and there may also be examples of subordinating conjunctions where appropriate. At times the language may be more basic than might otherwise be expected at this level. Overall the writing will be competent, mainly correct, but pedestrian.

Category	Mark	Content	Accuracy	Language Resource – Variety, Range, Structures
Satisfactory	6	◆ The candidate uses mainly simple, more basic sentences. ◆ The language is perhaps repetitive and uses a limited range of verbs and fixed phrases not appropriate to this level. ◆ The topic may not be fully addressed. ◆ In some cases, the content may be similar to that of good or very good examples, but with some serious accuracy issues.	◆ The verbs are generally correct, but basic. ◆ Tenses may be inconsistent. ◆ There are quite a few errors in other parts of speech – personal pronouns, gender of nouns, adjective endings, cases, singular/plural confusion – and in the use of accents. ◆ Some prepositions may be inaccurate or omitted e.g. I go the town. ◆ While the language may be reasonably accurate at times, the language structure may deteriorate significantly in places. ◆ Overall, there is more correct than incorrect and there is the impression overall that the candidate can handle tenses.	◆ The candidate copes with the present tense of most verbs. ◆ A limited range of verbs is used. ◆ Candidate relies on a limited range of vocabulary and structures. ◆ Where the candidate attempts constructions with modal verbs, these are not always successful. ◆ Sentences may be basic and mainly brief. ◆ There is minimal use of adjectives, probably mainly after 'is' e.g. My friend is reliable. ◆ The candidate has a weak knowledge of plurals. ◆ There may be several spelling errors e.g. reversal of vowel combinations.

Category	Mark	Content	Accuracy	Language Resource – Variety, Range, Structures
Unsatisfactory	4	◆ In some cases the content may be basic. ◆ In other cases there may be little difference in content between Satisfactory and Unsatisfactory. ◆ The language is repetitive, with undue reliance on fixed phrases and a limited range of common basic verbs such as *to be*, *to have*, *to play*, *to watch*. ◆ While the language used to address the more predictable aspects of the task may be accurate, serious errors occur when the candidate attempts to address a less predictable aspect. ◆ The Personal Response may be presented as a single paragraph.	◆ Ability to form tenses is inconsistent. ◆ In the use of the perfect tense the auxiliary verb is omitted on a number of occasions. ◆ There may be confusion between the singular and plural form of verbs. ◆ There are errors in many other parts of speech – gender of nouns, cases, singular/plural confusion – and in spelling and, where appropriate, word order. ◆ Several errors are serious, perhaps showing mother tongue interference. ◆ There may be one sentence which is not intelligible to a sympathetic native speaker. ◆ Overall, there is more incorrect than correct.	◆ The candidate copes mainly only with predictable language. ◆ There is inconsistency in the use of various expressions, especially verbs. ◆ Sentences are more basic. ◆ An English word may appear in the writing or a word may be omitted. ◆ There may be an example of serious dictionary misuse.

Category	Mark	Content	Accuracy	Language Resource – Variety, Range, Structures
Poor	2	◆ The content and language may be very basic. ◆ However, in many cases the content may be little different from that expected at Unsatisfactory or even at Satisfactory.	◆ Many of the verbs are incorrect or even omitted. ◆ There are many errors in other parts of speech – personal pronouns, gender of nouns, adjective endings, cases, singular/plural confusion – and in spelling and word order. ◆ Prepositions are not used correctly. ◆ The language is probably inaccurate throughout the writing. ◆ Some sentences may not be understood by a sympathetic native speaker.	◆ The candidate cannot cope with more than 1 or 2 basic verbs, frequently 'has' and 'is'. ◆ Verbs used more than once may be written differently on each occasion. ◆ The candidate has a very limited vocabulary. ◆ Several English or 'made-up' words may appear in the writing. ◆ There are examples of serious dictionary misuse.
Very Poor	0	◆ The content is very basic.	◆ (Virtually) nothing is correct. ◆ Most of the errors are serious. ◆ Very little is intelligible to a sympathetic native speaker.	◆ The candidate copes only with 'have' and 'am'. ◆ Very few words are correctly written in the foreign language. English words are used. ◆ There may be several examples of mother tongue interference. ◆ There may be several examples of serious dictionary misuse.

APPENDIX SIX: SPEAKING

Categories	Criteria	Pegged marks	
		Presentation	Discussion
Very Good	Confident handling of language with a high level of accuracy. Speaks fluently and without undue hesitation, or where there is some hesitation recovers well, and readily goes beyond minimal responses. Wide range of vocabulary and structures appropriate to Higher. Immediate and almost total understanding of almost everything said. Pronunciation and intonation sufficient to be readily under-stood by a speaker of the language.	10	15
Good	The language is mostly accurate, with a wide range of vocabulary and structures appropriate to this level. Speaks fluently and without undue hesitation, or where there is some hesitation recovers well, and generally goes beyond minimal responses. Understands almost everything said. Pronunciation and intonation sufficient to be generally understood by a speaker of the language.	8	12
Satisfactory	Completes task, demonstrating sufficient accuracy in a range of vocabulary and structures appropriate to this level, to convey meaning clearly, in spite of errors. May be hesitant and give only minimal correct responses or speak at greater length with less accuracy. Capable of coming to an understanding of all that is said. Pronunciation and intonation sufficient to be understood by a sympathetic speaker of the language.	6	9

Categories	Criteria	Pegged marks	
		Presentation	Discussion
Unsatisfactory (Near Miss)	Difficulty in achieving communication because of limited range of vocabulary and structures and/or serious inaccuracies in language appropriate to Higher. Understands most of what is said clearly and slowly by a sympathetic speaker. May speak with a considerable degree of hesitation, but makes some attempt to recover. Pronunciation and intonation sufficient to be generally understood by a sympathetic speaker of the language.	4	6
Poor	Communication seriously impeded by inadequate vocabulary and structures and/or by gross errors in language appropriate to Higher. Frequently has difficulty in understanding what is said, even with help. There may be occasional other tongue interference. Pronunciation and intonation may be such as to require clarification, even from a sympathetic speaker of the language.	2	3
Poor	No redeeming features.	0	0

Note: A total mark of 12 out of 25 equates to a 'Pass' for the unit, provided neither component falls below the 'Near Miss' category.